Naked

NOT YOUR AVERAGE SEX ENCYCLOPEDIA

Myriam Daguzan Bernier

illustrated by Cécile Gariépy

ORCA BOOK PUBLISHERS

Originally published in French in 2019 by
Les éditions Cardinal under the title *Tout nu!*
Le dictionnaire bienveillant de la sexualité.

Published in Canada and the United States
in 2022 by Orca Book Publishers.
orcabook.com

Library and Archives Canada
Cataloguing in Publication
Title: Naked : not your average sex encyclopedia
/ Myriam Daguzan Bernier ;
illustrations by Cécile Gariépy.
Other titles: Tout nu! English Names: Daguzan Bernier,
Myriam, author. | Gariépy, Cécile, illustrator. |
Simard, Charles, 1983– translator.
Description: Translation of: Tout nu! |
Translated by Charles Simard.
Identifiers: Canadiana (print) 20210255420 |
Canadiana (ebook) 20210255528 |
ISBN 9781459831018 (softcover) |
ISBN 9781459823143 (PDF) |
ISBN 9781459823150 (EPUB)
Subjects: LCSH: Sex instruction for teenagers—
Encyclopedias, Juvenile. | LCSH: Teenagers—
Sexual behavior—Encyclopedias, Juvenile. |
LCSH: Sex—Encyclopedias, Juvenile. |
LCSH: Human body—Encyclopedias, Juvenile. |
LCGFT: Encyclopedias.
Classification: LCC HQ35 .D3413 2022 |
DDC j306.70835/03—dc23

Library of Congress Control Number: 2020951466

Summary: This nonfiction encyclopedia
introduces teens to practical information about
sexuality from A to Z. It explains 155 body-
related terms and is illustrated throughout.

Orca Book Publishers is committed to
reducing the consumption of nonrenewable
resources in the production of our books.
We make every effort to use materials
that support a sustainable future.

Orca Book Publishers gratefully
acknowledges the support for its publishing
programs provided by the following agencies:
the Government of Canada, the Canada
Council for the Arts and the Province of
British Columbia through the BC Arts
Council and the Book Publishing Tax Credit.

We acknowledge the financial support
of the Government of Canada through
the National Translation Program for
Book Publishing, an initiative of the
*Roadmap for Canada's Official Languages
2013–2018: Education, Immigration,
Communities*, for our translation activities.

SODEC
Québec

We thank SODEC for its financial assistance.

Cover and interior artwork by Cécile Gariépy

Translated by Charles Simard

Printed and bound in South Korea.

25 24 23 22 • 1 2 3 4

To Pascal, for all that awaits us
To Guylaine, who brought me out of my shell

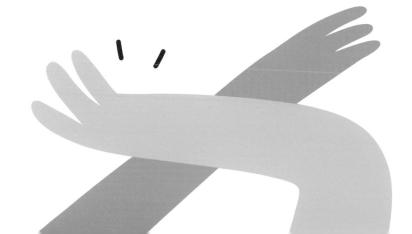

PREFACE
A LITTLE FUN, FOR CRYING OUT LOUD!*

I remember one afternoon spent at the public library when I was a teenager or young adult (it's blurry in my head). I was leafing through some anatomy manuals. In one of those books—the title of which escapes me completely—a chapter that raised the question of gender particularly interested me. It explained how researchers had experimented with children who had been brought up having a gender different from the sex assigned to them at birth—a girl "raised as a boy" and a boy "raised as a girl"—and how that had transformed their bodies. I was both fascinated and horrified. I learned, in another part of the same book, that people with serious kidney problems (I'm one of these people) were more likely to develop male traits or suffer from disorders of sex development (this was certainly a chapter about *intersex* people). I was dumbfounded. Did that mean I was a bit of a "man"? Did that explain why at times I didn't feel I fit in a "woman's role"? And why I felt stuck in the attitudes and codes that are so often imposed on girls? Was it for the same reason that, when I did act as an "ultrafeminine" woman (say, in my choice of clothes, makeup or in my body language), I sometimes felt like I was "dressing up"?

Obviously, at the time I was confusing a lot of different concepts (biological sex, gender expression, gender identity, gender stereotypes and so on), but that reading had a lasting effect on me: something inside me made me "nonstandard." But then, what was "standard"? What was "normal"? I didn't know. Having always had problems with my period, coupled with the regular appearance of cysts and strange shapes that changed with each ultrasound I was given, I remember wondering if I would one day be told by the doctor that instead of an ovary I had...a testicle! And my strenuous

* Title inspired by the 2007 dance show *Un peu de tendresse bordel de merde!* (*A little tenderness for crying out loud!*) by choreographer Dave St-Pierre.

gynecological follow-ups never really succeeded in convincing me I was completely "normal"—whatever that meant. When I found out (although it wasn't much of a surprise, to be honest) that one of my former boyfriends was gay, I had so many questions! I realized over time that attractions, and many other things, can fluctuate and change during a lifetime. That there are *many* sexualities and many ways to experience sexuality. There is, in fact, a rainbow of possibilities, through which multiple identities and sexual orientations can unfold. I realized there existed a beautiful, multicolored umbrella under which I took refuge and understood that each person has their journey sown with doubts and fears but also discoveries. And that it can be both interesting *and* important to talk about sexuality.

Long story short, I wrote this book thinking of the teenager I once was, one who asked herself a lot of questions (and I haven't changed since!). Questions about her gender, her breasts, her buttocks, her whole body, the "normal" age to do this or that, how guys and girls "work," how to deal with sexuality—a subtle balance between "seeming to like it" but not liking it too much, so as not to pass for an "easy" girl—when in fact I didn't know the first thing about all these things! I wish the teenager I was had been told that nothing is all black or all white. That identities don't restrict themselves to just two closed groups. That sexual orientations are diverse and fluctuating. That when your "first time" comes, you shouldn't care how old you are, because there will be loads of firsts anyway.

I wish I had been told that a fulfilling sex life has nothing to do with finding the perfect body. That you can have fun and laugh about it, that sex isn't a performance and you don't have to take it seriously all the time. That there are as many ways to experience sexuality as there are people on the planet, because every sexual relationship is unique. That sexuality is not an act that you can "copy and paste," the same way every day. That it can be great one day and not so great the next. That it can be limited to hugs and that's fine. That penetration is just *one* of many ways to have fun. That you can say no. Or say yes and then change your mind. That the sexuality depicted in the movies is so different from what you'll experience in real life. That sexuality is important, but that you can also choose to do without it. That sexuality can be the least of your worries, and even something that doesn't appeal to you at all, and that's fine too.

As a teenager, I asked myself so many questions and got so few answers. I wish I could have had access to a guilt-free, open and reassuring conversation that allowed people to be who they are or want to be. A conversation that gave people the right to say, "I don't like it" and "I don't have to do this or that." That allowed people to choose their own sexuality or sexualities. That's how I came up with the idea for this book—a heartwarming book, an open book, a book to make people reach out and ask, "How about we talk about it?"

I study sexology and have been interested in sexuality for a long time, especially as a journalist. It's my passion for the subject and for human relations in general that prompted me to write this book. Sex is at the heart of our social interactions and stereotypes, our identity, our gender expression, our romantic and friendly relationships, our perceptions of our bodies. Many discussions out there try to define what sexuality *should* be. But I wanted to think about this topic a little more and talk about it openly, without judgment.

So I created this encyclopedia. *Naked* is a practical guide that can be read from start to finish, from finish to start, or in any way you see fit. It doesn't have all the answers, but I think it may contain a few. Above all, it's a book that prompts you to open doors and look further.

I hope this book may be a friend, a companion, to you.

I want to be an ally. I think we need to stop and listen to what is being said about sexuality and sexualities. Because each one of us is unique and because knowing about other people's perspectives and experiences in life can only be beneficial. Let's make the world a better place, dare I say!

I have a simple word of guidance
for you while you're
reading this book:
Have *fun*.

Adolescence

Noun, from Latin *adolescere*, "to grow, come to maturity"

The word *adolescence* means "the process or state of growing up." In other words, it means you're going somewhere or moving toward something. It refers to an important stage in life.

Big changes are happening during this time! It's called **puberty**. From a hormonal standpoint, the body is very active. Changes occur on the physical level. The body is transformed, taking shape and gaining muscle. Between ages 6 and 11, children double their weight, and between 12 and 18, they go through an extraordinary growth spurt. Voices break, hair starts to grow on the face and in unexpected places, breasts get larger, penises get longer...everything is transformed! It can be weird and unsettling. Teenagers also go through psychological changes. They become more independent, define their personalities, make choices.

And everyone changes at their own pace. Biologically speaking, the bodies of people with a female sex undergo significant changes around the age of 9 or 10, while the bodies of people with a male sex change around the age of 11 or 12. But it doesn't happen at the same time for everyone. In some cases, puberty can be "advanced" or "delayed." An increasing number of young girls today experience precocious puberty, which means that the process for them can start when they are as young as 7 years old! What does that mean? Several things, including this: girls with precocious puberty reach sexual maturity early in their lives.

Adolescence has long been regarded as a difficult time in a person's life, but for most people, it goes quite smoothly. Nobody turns into a monster or a vegetable during their teens. On the contrary, in fact. It's during this period that the capacity for abstract thought—also called hypothetico-deductive reasoning (say what?)—usually emerges. In other words, during adolescence a person becomes able to deduce things, form hypotheses (and therefore better understand how other people think) and grasp abstract concepts such as justice.

A STORM IS COMING

In the late 1800s Anna Freud, the renowned psychoanalyst and daughter of the famous founder of psychoanalysis, Sigmund Freud, compared adolescence to a kind of storm, a tidal wave characterized by contradictory states: "Adolescents engage with passion in intense romantic relationships but abandon them as unexpectedly as they started them. On the one hand, they enthusiastically engage in the life of the community and, on the other hand, they feel an all-powerful desire for isolation. They oscillate between blind submission to any leader and rebellion defying all authority. They are selfish and materialistic but at the same time prove to be overflowing with exalted idealism. They are ascetic, but they succumb, unexpectedly, to the most basic instinctive excesses."

Today we know that the prefrontal cortex in the adolescent brain isn't fully developed. That can impede decision-making, and combined with hormonal changes can cause extreme behaviors.

Agender

Adjective, from Greek privative prefix *a-* (*á-*), "without,"
and Latin *genus*, "origin, type, group"

In our society, we divide people into two groups, men and women. These labels, given to us at birth on the basis of our biological sex, dictate what gender we belong to (see **gender-neutral**). But gender is much more complex than that. Many people don't feel like they're either men or women and are uncomfortable being forced into one of these categories. They want to break away from it. When someone is agender, it means they reject the idea of gender. An agender (or nongendered, genderless or genderfree) person wants to be recognized as neither male nor female, as a person without a gender. It's an important decision that makes them feel better about their social and intimate life, their body and their mind. And it's just as important that we respect their decision.

Can you be agender and have a sexuality? Absolutely. Being agender has nothing to do with **asexuality**.

Alexithymia

Noun, from Greek *a*-, "without," *lexis*, "speech" and *thumos*, "emotion, soul"

....

Alexithymia is a disorder characterized by difficulty finding the words to express emotions, meaning they are repressed and kept within. People with alexithymia tend to isolate themselves, avoid facing their emotions and can't explain what's going on inside them. And when they do manage to express themselves, alexithymic people may succeed in describing concrete facts or even physical symptoms but still struggle linking them to specific emotions.

There are a number of ways you can do it. For some people, it's easier to express emotions in writing—keeping a diary, for example. For others, they might cope with their emotions through physical activity, say, by jogging to let off some steam. Others may prefer meditating. You might even find that browsing through an encyclopedia—;)—helps you find the words that correspond to your moods. Why not?

Up to 10 percent of the general population is believed to be alexithymic.

Up to 10 percent of the general population is believed to be alexithymic.

Many people think that women express themselves more and better than men do. But this isn't true. Emotions are fundamentally human and have no sex or gender. Regardless of sex or gender, it is important to be able to explore and express your emotions.

Ally

Noun, from Old French *alie*, "allied," based on the
verb from Latin, *alligare*, "bind together"

An ally is someone who, when witnessing some form of injustice, chooses to defend the person or group of people being targeted. For example, an ally may speak out to defend the rights of minority groups* and to reduce inequalities. Minority groups include trans people, nonbinary people, people with excess weight, people with disabilities, members of the LGBTQQIP2SAA+ community, People of Color and economically underprivileged people. Allies typically have good listening skills, show empathy, have a good understanding of different types of oppression and are aware of their own privilege.

Although the initialism LGBTQQIP2SAA+ includes a second *A* for *ally*, not everyone agrees that it should. Even though allies stand beside LGBTQQIP2SAA+ people to fight against discrimination, they don't experience the same oppression these communities do. The support that allies give minority groups is necessary and important, but only the people in minority communities have intimate knowledge of the discrimination and stigmatization they face.

Racism, ableism, sexism, classism—in *Is Everyone Really Equal? An Introduction to Key Concepts in Social Justice Education*, authors Özlem Sensoy and Robin DiAngelo explain where various types of oppression come from and how they work. It's a great reference for anyone interested in understanding the inequalities that exist in our society.

* Caution: The fact that a so-called minority group is stigmatized and oppressed doesn't mean that it is "in the minority." Minority groups can consist of a significant number of people and still be perceived as a minority, as part of the "margin," and therefore can still be marginalized.

Anal Sex

Anal: adjective, from Latin *analis*, "concerning the anus," from *anus*, "a ring"
Sex: noun, from Latin *sexus*, "sex, gender"

Even though it was widely practiced in places like ancient Greece and Rome, anal sex has had bad press for centuries. Until very recently, the Canadian Criminal Code prohibited anal sex. It was illegal except when conducted in private between consenting adults 18 or older, or between a husband and wife. Prime Minister Justin Trudeau introduced Bill C-32 in November 2016, which abolishes the section in question. The bill has been ratified, but its application is subject to interpretation.

Yet anal sex is nothing more than one way among others to experience pleasure. And it's now a common practice, regardless of sexual orientation.

Sexuality isn't limited to a man and a woman practicing vaginal penetration. That's "normalized" sexuality of the sort we're constantly shown in movies, books, TV shows and magazines. But there are many other ways you can experience your sexuality. And anal sex is one of them. Sexuality is a field of exploration.

When people talk about anal sex, they usually mean a penis, one (or more) fingers or even an object, such as a vibrator, penetrating the anus. But the anus is an **erogenous zone**, meaning an area that can generate **arousal**. The anus can also be touched and caressed (using one or more fingers, a sex toy or a penis) without any penetration coming into play. Kisses and caresses with the tongue and mouth can also take place, a practice called anilingus or, colloquially, rimming.

ANAL SEX OR SODOMY?

The word *sodomy* is sometimes used to refer to anal sex. But anal sex and sodomy didn't always mean the same thing. *Sodomy* comes from the biblical story of Sodom and Gomorrah, two cities destroyed by Yahweh in the Old Testament because their inhabitants had allegedly tried to rape angels that were sent to earth. The word came to refer to many things throughout history, including bestiality (having sexual relations with an animal), a sexual activity experienced for pleasure (a forbidden notion until recently, since sexuality was for a long time understood to be a way to make babies) and even masturbation, alone or with other partners. Nowadays it's associated more with anal penetration. The term *anal sex* more clearly defines what's going on and, most important, contains no judgments associated with its definition.

Anal sex is an intimate gesture that requires consent and must be discussed with your partner(s). Take your time. Prepare for it! If you want to enjoy the experience of anal penetration, you have to be relaxed (don't do it just to please your partner) and, ideally, do it with someone you trust. Lubricant is a great tool to have around when you're having anal sex. And the use of a **dental dam** makes it possible to avoid direct contact between the anus and your mouth and tongue, if you're not sure of your partner's sexual past. **STDs** (sexually transmitted diseases) or **STIs** (sexually transmitted infections) can be avoided in this way.

Listen to your tastes and desires, and have fun! But above all: You. Don't. Have. To.

ANAL CHRISTMAS TREE?

Paris, 2014. A scandal erupted when an artwork by the American artist Paul McCarthy was installed on the famous Place Vendôme. McCarthy's *Tree*, a sort of gigantic inflatable Christmas tree, looked very much like...a butt plug (or anal plug), a conical sex toy used to masturbate or give pleasure. The artwork was vandalized and dismantled only two days after its installation.

BYE-BYE, PREJUDICES AND TABOOS!

"Gay men all have anal sex."
FALSE. It's a personal choice. And anal sex isn't related to sex, gender or sexual orientation. People practice it because they want to, with whomever they love or like, and regardless of their sexual identity. That's it, that's all!

"It's 'gay' for a straight man to enjoy anal sex and to be penetrated."
SUPER FALSE. Just because a male person enjoys anal sex doesn't mean that anything can be inferred about their sexual orientation. The former has absolutely nothing to do with the latter. And take note that in males, the perineum, located between the anus and the scrotum, is an erogenous zone. Because of such prejudices, many men prevent themselves from discovering another source of pleasure.

"If I don't feel like having anal sex, I'm close-minded."
FALSE, FALSE, FALSE. If you say you don't like ice cream, do people have the right to tell you to be more open and loosen up a bit? No. To each their own. That's all. Don't feel like having anal sex? Then you don't, and that's it.

Anorexia and Reverse Anorexia

Anorexia: noun, from Greek *anorexia*, "without appetite,"
from *an-*, "without," and *orexis*, "appetite"
Reverse: adjective, from Old French *revers*, "a change of direction"

In August 2018, a video on Instagram went viral. It showed the Kardashian sisters congratulating Kim on her recent weight loss, using the word *anorexic* as a compliment. After being told she must have gone without food to reach that size, Kim replies, "Oh my god, thank you!"—thereby suggesting that not eating is, first, a good thing and, second, the perfect diet solution.

Contrary to what the Kardashians displayed in that video, anorexia is a serious eating disorder. Those who suffer from it experience drastic weight loss primarily by severe dieting and prolonged periods of fasting. Other people make themselves vomit after meals or use laxatives to keep them from gaining weight after eating (see **bulimia**). According to Statistics Canada, women are affected by eating disorders 10 times more than men are. According to a study by the National Eating Disorders Association (NEDA), "approximately 20 million females and 10 million males in the US have a clinically significant eating disorder at some point in their lifetime."

The Douglas Mental Health University Institute in Montreal says anorexia can be caused by several factors, including heredity, as eating disorders can be passed from one generation to the next, and the social pressure created by beauty standards. It points out that anorexia is often accompanied by **anxiety** disorders and impulse-control disorders, which make some people unable to control their relationship with food.

ADDICTED TO THE GYM

While people with anorexia never find themselves thin enough, others never find their muscles big enough. The latter is called reverse anorexia, muscle dysmorphia or bigorexia. It's the practice of training excessively to achieve a muscle mass that's out of proportion to the body. People with this condition may become addicted to training to the point of isolating themselves from their circle of friends and making themselves sick.

The good news is that there is help available. The National Eating Disorder Information Centre (NEDIC) offers support to people who suffer from anorexia and **bulimia**. See nedic.ca. There's also a National Eating Disorders Awareness Week in Canada, which aims to inform people about the causes of these disorders and dispel the myths surrounding them. The National Eating Disorders Association (NEDA) is an American nonprofit organization dedicated to preventing and managing eating disorders. See nationaleatingdisorders.org.

Anxiety

Noun, from Latin *anxietas*, "anxiety, anguish"

According to the Douglas Mental Health University Institute, anxiety is "a biological mechanism whose function is to protect us from dangerous situations." It's therefore normal to experience some form of anxiety when faced with unknown or uncertain situations—it's a human protective reflex. But although it has a purpose, anxiety can become problematic, and even pathological, if it prevents you from functioning normally in life.

More and more children and teenagers are living with significant anxiety problems. Whether it's performance anxiety, separation anxiety, generalized anxiety, social phobia, panic attacks or post-traumatic stress disorder (PTSD), anxiety disorders have been on the rise in young people for the past 15 years.

Stress before school exams, fear of being separated from your parents, phobia about certain social situations (going to school, having to confront classmates, etc.) or even fear of dying or of an impending event…all are kinds of anxiety disorders. And they're not easy to manage. That's why you shouldn't hesitate to seek help or talk to people you trust if you experience anxiety.

When you come out of your isolation, you'll quickly realize that you're not the only one living with anxiety. It's important to share tips on how to overcome these difficulties and learn to better manage anxiety.

PERFORMANCE ANXIETY

People often have expectations about sex—that it should be frequent, exciting, available on demand and fulfilling every time. But the reality can be quite different, and such expectations can cause performance anxiety, which is apprehension or stress about sex.

WHO TO TALK TO IF THINGS GO WRONG:

> a trusted family member
> a close friend
> a teacher you get along with
> a psychologist
> a doctor
> a helpline such as Kids Help Phone, 1-800-668-6868 or kidshelpphone.ca (Canada only), or Teen Line, teenlineonline.org (North America)

App

Application: noun, from Old French *application*, "act of applying something"

Most of us use a smartphone or tablet every day to communicate, get information, play and so on. These devices can also be practical tools for a lot of other things, such as updating your schedule or monitoring your **menstrual cycle**. If you're the type to have your nose glued to your phone a lot of the time, why not also use it to take care of your body and your sexuality?

But before you get started make informed decisions and check with friends or adults you trust about which apps they use. Check the small print to see if the app stores your personal data and decide if you feel okay about this.

GET HELP

Several support organizations are active on social media and easily accessible. They cover a variety of topics—violence, harassment, intimidation, sexual assault, pregnancy, contraception, STDs or STIs, etc. With most organizations, you can ask your questions anonymously (as with Kids Help Phone, for example). Many mobile apps offer help for a variety of situations, such as +FORT, which offers support in cases of bullying. See centreaxel.com/en/projects/stronger-than-bullying

AlterHéros is an online community committed to fighting prejudice and demystifying sexual diversity and gender plurality. It offers the opportunity to anonymously ask questions related to sexual orientation, gender identity, gender expression or sexual health. For the benefit of everyone, questions and answers are shared online. See alterheros.com/en/home

AT YOUR FINGERTIPS...

Learn about sexuality

YouTube showcases a lot of great content on sexuality, sexual health or, more generally, the human body. Many YouTubers specialize in these fields and answer questions well—questions like, "Is my vulva normal?" and "What method should I use to manage my period?" and "How are babies made?"

About Sex is a series by CBC Gem on YouTube: cbc.ca/mediacentre/program/about-sex

Hannah Witton, an inclusive and super-open English YouTuber, discusses issues related to sexuality: youtube.com/user/hannahgirasol

Shan Boodram is an American sexologist and intimacy expert: youtube.com/user/shannontboodram

Ash Hardell is a creative YouTuber and author who discusses gender identities and the LGBTQQIP2SAA+ community: youtube.com/user/HeyThere005

Scarleteen.com includes inclusive, comprehensive and supportive sexuality and relationship information for teens and emerging adults.

Manage your periods and contraceptive methods

Several apps allow you to follow your menstrual cycle and monitor your "fertile window," so you can know when to carry sanitary products with you and when the risk of becoming pregnant is the highest.

Glow

glowing.com/glow
(free, for iOS and Android)

Natural Cycles

naturalcycles.com/en
(paid, for iOS and Android)

Spot On Period Tracker

plannedparenthood.org/get-care/spot-on-period-tracker
(free, for iOS and Android)

Clue

helloclue.com
(free and paid versions, for iOS and Android)

Flo

flo.health
(free, for iOS and Android)

MagicGirl

magicgirl.me
(free, for iOS and Android)

Aromantic

Adjective, from Greek privative prefix *a-*, "without," and French *romantique*, "pertaining to the romantic literary genre"

When people talk about romance and romanticism, they usually think of passionate love. But for some people, the feeling of love doesn't mean much. They don't feel the need to love or be loved and don't want to be lovingly, "romantically" involved with a partner. This preference is called aromanticism. People who prefer this way of managing their relationships are described as *aromantic*.

But be careful—it's possible to be aromantic, and therefore not involved in a romantic relationship, but still have sex with other people. Just because you're aromantic doesn't mean you're also *asexual* (see **asexuality**). Those are two different things.

Arousal

Noun, from the verb *to rouse*, "to wake up"

Some signs don't lie when a person is sexually aroused: muscle tension (you become more tense), accelerated heart rate and breathing (your heart is pounding), erect penis, hardened nipples, sweating, activated vagina's Bartholin's glands, which secrete a lubricating liquid aimed to facilitate penetration (see **lubrication**).

Know that while the physical signs of sexual arousal are similar from one person to another, what goes on in your head (your sexual thoughts, for example) could be very different from someone else's thoughts. Something that turns you on may not turn on the person next to you at all—what's exciting for a person is relative and intimate.

Asexuality

Noun, from Greek privative prefix *a-*, "without," and Latin *sexualis*, "sexual," from *sexus*, "sex, gender"

Sexual desire is complex, intimate and experienced differently by each person. While some people have attractions to all genders, some may have attraction to certain gender expressions, which might change and be fluid over time. These people are said to be asexual.

According to the Asexual Visibility and Education Network (AVEN), 1 percent of the world's population is asexual. That means in Canada, there are more than 375,000 asexual people.

Nonetheless, a person can be asexual and still have sex as well as desire a romantic relationship *without* being sexually attracted to someone. *Asexuality* and *aromanticism* are not the same at all.

How do you know if you're asexual? The Asexual Visibility and Education Network (AVEN) website explains that asexuality is difficult to detect, that we all experience things differently and must reflect on ourselves. It's up to every individual to make their own way in asexuality. See asexuality.org.

BATHROOM
BEAUTY
BIOLOGICAL SEX
BISEXUALITY
BODY
BODY DYSMORPHIA
BODY HAIR
BODY IMAGE
BODY-SHAMING
BRA
BREASTS
BULIMIA
BUTTOCKS

B

Bathroom

Bath: Noun, from Old English *baeth*
Room: Noun, from the Middle English *roum*

In recent years, several LGBTQQIP2SAA+ groups have been campaigning for public places to offer mixed-sex or **gender-neutral** bathrooms. It's time for the female and male symbols on the doors to evolve! Gender-neutral bathrooms are for anyone to use, regardless of their gender and sex.

The topic of gender-neutral facilities has sparked intense debate over the past few years. Considered a whim by some people, they're a matter of health and safety for others, especially trans and nonbinary people.

Believe it or not, bathrooms are often the site of violent verbal and physical exchanges. In an American study carried out in 2013 on the minority stress (see **stress**) that trans people experience as a result of the male/female separation of public bathrooms, 70 percent of respondents said they had been harassed or assaulted in a bathroom.

GENDER POO

In 2008 queer artist Coco Guzman, aka Coco Riot, created an installation called *Genderpoo* in which signs like those used in public bathrooms are transformed into signs of inclusion. Guzman's work is aimed at questioning the man/woman binary norms imposed by society. Read more at cocoriot.com/cocoart#/genderpoo.

BATHROOMS FOR EVERYBODY!

Many places, such as schools, universities and colleges, have already adopted gender-neutral bathrooms (also called unisex, gender-inclusive, mixed-sex and all-gender bathrooms), thereby promoting a climate of safety for all.

Beauty

Noun, from Modern French *beauté*, "beauty," from
Latin *bellus*, "beautiful, pleasant"

Beauty is a relative concept. What is considered beautiful today might not have been by yesterday's standards. Each era creates its own standards of beauty. For example, in the 19th century, very pale, almost cadaveric skin tones were in fashion. Some 19th-century tips for maintaining super-pale skin? Try drinking vinegar and depriving yourself of sleep!

A slim waist, however, wasn't always fashionable. According to French historian and sociologist Georges Vigarello, a specialist in the evolution of body practices throughout history, fashion trends after World War II were all about curves. Vigarello's hypothesis was that after being deprived of food during the war, people were traumatized and found the sight of plump bodies comforting. And comforting bodies meant maternal figures, an image that was reentering the collective imagination at that time.

> What is considered beautiful today might not have been by yesterday's standards.

Today, bodies idealized in advertisements exude health, in addition to being tanned, lean and athletic.

What is considered beautiful also varies from person to person and between cultures. You may find a person very beautiful while your best friend feels the opposite way. Very often it's by getting to know someone and spending time with them that you end up finding them beautiful. There are as many types of beauty as there are individuals. It might be a cliché, but it's true: beauty goes beyond skin-deep.

Round. Sensual. Vivid. Exalted. Words such as these words are often used to describe the voluminous bodies painted and sculpted by the Colombian artist Fernando Botero. Botero's bodies represent for the artist "an exaltation of life, a sensuality." Magnificent bodies, indeed!

Biological Sex

Biological: adjective, from *biology* (from German *Biologie*, from Greek *bios*)
Sex: noun, from Latin *sexus*, "sex, gender"

Each person is born with a biological sex, which can be female, male or **intersex**. Sex, or sex assigned at birth, is a medical and legal distinction that determines whether a newborn child falls into the category of male or female. However, these binary definitions don't take into account the sexual realities of intersex and trans people.

Biological sex is noted on children's birth certificates, as well as various legal documents, such as driver's licenses and passports. Recently some Canadian provinces have started offering nonbinary sex designations on birth certificates. Many US states also offer gender-neutral birth certificates (see **gender-neutral**). An official change of sex can also be made on Canadian passports.

Bisexuality

Noun, from Latin *bi-*, "two," and *sexualis*, "sexual"

Being bisexual means a person is attracted to both women and men. But this definition is a bit reductive, because it takes for granted that there are only two genders (male and female), whereas **gender** and gender **identity** include many more nuances and possibilities.

A bisexual person can be attracted to both sexes but only one gender—feminine or masculine people, for example. More specifically, some people may be attracted to all sexes but prefer a partner with a more feminine attitude who isn't necessarily a woman or, conversely, someone more masculine but who isn't a man.

Other people prefer to say they're attracted to one specific *person*, regardless of their gender or sex. This is called **pansexuality**.

BI-CURIOUS?

Some people say they are bi-curious, meaning they don't wish to identify as bisexual, but they are curious to explore sexual, emotional or romantic relationships with people of a sex different from the one they usually prefer.

Body

Noun, from Old English *bodig*, "body, chest, torso"

The body is a complex and fascinating machine that carries us during the entirety of our lives. But when we're teenagers, we sometimes feel like it's letting us down, laughing at us or acting silly! This is normal, because at this point in our lives, our bodies are changing tremendously and over a very short time. Think about it for a moment. In just a few years, people go from childhood to adulthood, inside what will be their body shell for most of their lives. Mind-boggling! So why not try to understand your body as soon as possible? Love it, accept it and — especially in the context of sexuality — know how it works and feels.

Try to understand and explore your body, so that you can love it better and discover your desires and preferences.

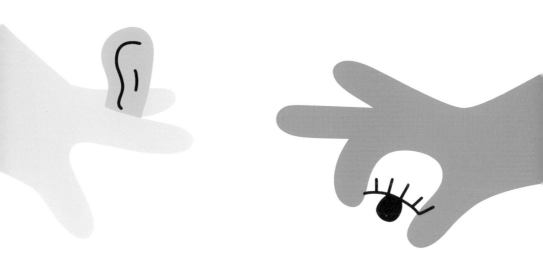

Body Dysmorphia
or Body Dysmorphic Disorder (BDD)

Body: noun, from Old English *bodig*, "trunk of a man or beast"
Dysmorphia: noun, from Greek *dusmorphia,* "misshapenness, ugliness"

Many of us spend a lot of time looking in the mirror to assess how we look. This behavior isn't surprising, given the importance society places on body image and what the ideal body should look like—usually thin, young, cisgender and able. Regardless of whether you meet the beauty standards portrayed in mainstream media, you're likely interested in your outside appearance and how others perceive you.

For a person living with BDD, body image becomes all-consuming. They are convinced their body and outward appearance have major flaws. Their perception of their own body is distorted and doesn't correspond to reality, causing them suffering and distress. Excessive behaviors that people with BDD may manifest include constantly comparing themselves to others, spending a lot of time in front of the mirror and, in some cases, resorting to cosmetic surgery.

Body Hair

Body: noun, from Old English *bodig*
Hair: noun, from Old English *hær*

September 2017. Young Swedish model and artist Arvida Byström does a photo shoot for a famous brand and the image clearly shows the hair on her legs. She receives threats of all kinds for having dared to display unshaven legs.

As crazy as the story sounds, it shows just how taboo and despised female body hair is in our society. Consider the trendiness of the laser hair-removal industry, or look at the pharmacy shelves stocked with hair-removal products. Many men too dislike their body hair, whether on their eyebrows, chest, armpits or even the pubic area. The hatred for "unsightly hair" seems boundless.

Humans probably said goodbye to most of their body hair approximately 114,000 years ago. The reason? To prevent parasites, such as lice, from settling in human "fur" and spreading diseases.

Over the centuries, the idea of doing away with the remaining body hair slowly made its way into society in order to differentiate humans from nonhuman animals, and human intelligence and evolution from those of other animals.

And yet body hair is full of virtues! Pubic hair, for example, can increase tactile and epidermal sensations during sex. It protects the epidermis (the outer layer of your skin) and prevents unwanted bacteria from entering the female genitals. Shaving your pubic hair may cause ingrown hairs, redness, itching and small lesions that increase your risk of getting an STD or STI. That said, a decrease in pubic lice in people who safely remove their pubic hair has been noticed.

Whether you're pro body hair or not, the fact remains that body hair has its uses, and it's important to know where the beauty standards that dictate which type of hair is acceptable and which isn't come from. Maybe one day we'll proudly display bushy armpits or nose hair extensions (yep, they really exist!).

JANUHAIRY

Since 2019, UK student and activist Laura Jackson has encouraged women not to shave their body hair throughout the month of January (renamed for the occasion as "Januhairy"). Jackson believes that hairy or not, we should accept ourselves as we are.

"Growing my body hair and accepting that part of myself was such a huge eye-opener," she says. "Not only to the taboo of body hair on women, but also how I view my own body. And it is such a huge challenge loving yourself every single day, but it's such an important thing to connect to yourself." For Jackson, there's nothing more natural than body hair!

Body Image

Body: noun, from Old English *bodig*, "body"
Image: noun, from Old French *image*, "image,
sight," from Latin *imago*, "copy, image"

Body image—the way you see your own body—is one of the most important components of self-esteem. It has an impact on your physical and mental health, the friendships you develop, your romantic relationships, the way you are and behave in society, your sexuality and so on.

In adolescence, body image takes on paramount importance, since you're greatly influenced by peers, the media and also, at times, family and friends, who might be perpetuating physical stereotypes. Sometimes parents make comments about their child's physical appearance and, without realizing it, teach them that their body doesn't meet socially accepted standards.

Teenagers also constantly wonder if their body, their clothes, their look are acceptable in the eyes of others. Am I muscular enough? Am I too fat? (See **fat talk** and **muscle talk**.) This is normal—there's a great need for validation during adolescence. Besides, these habits often remain with people into adulthood.

What's important—but not necessarily easy—is to ask yourself, Am I comfortable in my own skin, despite the standards of beauty that surround and pressure me, despite my body not being exactly as I would like it to be? When I wake up in the morning, do I feel good about myself? The answer's yes? Great! You appreciate who you are and what you have. The answer is no? Then what can you do to feel better, to feel beautiful and to appreciate who you are and how you look?

Learning to look at yourself with kindness and appreciate what you have is something to work on every day. Easy? Not necessarily. Feasible? You bet! Surrounding yourself with people who make you feel loved and appreciated, and who see your strengths and qualities, is a big step forward. It's also a good idea to take part in sports and social activities and have personal projects that make you feel good and build your confidence. Remember, **beauty** is relative. Our personalities are what make us look good or beautiful in the eyes of others.

> Surrounding yourself with people who make you feel loved and appreciated, and who see your strengths and qualities, is a big step forward.

Weight

Our society values being thin. When people think about sexuality, the images that typically come to mind are perfect bodies, ideally young, attractive and, above all, thin. It's as if obese or overweight people have no sexuality, or that their sexuality shouldn't be discussed because it doesn't conform to societal norms.

But everyone, regardless of their weight, has the right to experience desire, to have a beautiful, fulfilling and healthy sexuality...and to show it!

HEALTHY WEIGHT

We're constantly being reminded that a healthy weight based on the body mass index (BMI) is very important, but this famous calculation has its limits. According to Extenso, the center for nutrition at the University of Montreal, people should focus more on healthy habits than on weight: "Adopting healthy eating habits does not automatically lead to achieving a 'healthy weight' as defined by the BMI." A person can be overweight or even fat and nonetheless be in good health, and likewise a person can be thin and in poor health.

PERCEPTION PROBLEM?

A 2015 study published in the journal *Adolescent Health, Medicine and Therapeutics* showed that teen boys tend to be very concerned about their bodies and consider themselves overweight even when their BMIs are well within the normal range.

This finding confirmed the results of another study, carried out in 2002, which found that "two-thirds of high-school girls are dissatisfied with their figure, despite the fact that half of them are of normal weight."

Body-Shaming

Body: noun, from Old English *bodig*
Shaming: noun, from Old English *sc(e)amu*, "shame,"
and *sc(e)amian*, "to feel shame"

Body-shaming is the act of making degrading comments about a person's physical appearance or size to make them feel ashamed of their own body. Unfortunately almost everyone has experienced it at some point in their lives, regardless of gender, and the impact of this serious act can be disastrous on mental and physical health.

#THEYSAID

On May 25, 2017, Sally Bergesen, the CEO of a women's sports clothing company, posted a tweet in which she briefly recounted how her father first body-shamed her when she was 12, telling her, "Keep eating like that and you're going to be a butterball."

Bergesen used the hashtag #TheySaid and invited her subscribers to share their first body-shaming experience. Dozens and dozens of testimonies were posted, mostly coming from women, about disturbing experiences that all triggered a sense of shame about their bodies.

For these people, publicly sharing these past humiliations, and the violent nature of some of the insults thrown at them, allowed them to be heard, to feel understood and to interact with other victims of body-shaming. They could not only regain a sense of power for themselves but also educate others who may not have experienced body-shaming about the negative consequences of this practice on a person's self-esteem.

Bra

Noun, abbreviation of *brassiere*, from French *brassière*,
"a woman's or child's vest," from *bras*, "an arm"

....

Who hasn't heard of 1960s and 1970s feminists burning their bras to denounce patriarchy?* Well, that's a myth. It never happened.

In fact, in 1968 women marching in New York against the Miss America beauty contest threw their bras into a "freedom trash can" that was meant for all feminine objects symbolic of oppression. A less radical gesture, but still a striking one. The media at the time reported the news extensively and unwittingly fueled the collective imagination. Burning bras have been associated with feminism ever since.

But women have been claiming the right not to wear bras for a long while. Their arguments? First, they ask, why would female breasts be sexualized but not male ones? Second, while women with a large bust might feel more comfortable wearing a bra, studies have shown that bras don't ensure the perkiness of breasts—assuming breast firmness is a requirement (which it isn't). In fact, wearing a bra would tend to make breasts *less* firm. So why wear one?

Even today, some people wear a bra at night for fear that their breasts may lose firmness if they aren't supported. In fact, with age the body inevitably loses some of its firmness, and breasts are no exception to the general

rule—they will descend slowly, thanks to gravity. Unfortunately, as the media hammers home the message that firm breasts are the most beautiful, "sexy" and "normal" trait on a woman's body, many people take every possible precaution to avoid developing sagging breasts. Even sleeping in a bra.

Long story short, you have the right to decide whether to get rid of your bra or to keep wearing one because it makes you feel better. The important thing is to feel good about yourself and make the decision that suits you, not others.

GOODBYE, SEXIST DRESS CODES!

In March 2018 in Montreal, a young woman was asked by the principal of her school to hide her breasts, supposedly highlighted by the absence of a bra. Several students showed their support for the young woman by coming to school without wearing bras. The school listened to the students' demands, and wearing a bra is no longer mandatory at the school.

* Patriarchy is the social organization of a family, government or community designed to give men the decision-making power in several spheres of society, including politics, religion and the economy. The word was taken up by feminists in the 1970s to denounce the oppression of women.

Breasts

Noun, from Old English *brēost*, "mammary gland of a woman, bosom"

Why are female breasts so scrutinized, analyzed and criticized? Why do girls hide their emerging breasts? Why are girls taught at an early age to be self-conscious about their breasts and to feel guilty when they don't hide them adequately?

And what about the taboo against public breastfeeding? A lot of people are still uncomfortable with women breastfeeding in public. In 2015 celebrities, including Alyssa Milano and Alanis Morissette, shared "brelfies" — *breasts + selfie* — on Instagram to promote the fact that breastfeeding is completely natural and shouldn't be frowned upon.

In our society, female breasts are sexualized. Why is that? Scientists don't agree on the reasons, but they have a few hypotheses. One is that breasts are a sign of fertility — their primary biological function is to nourish offspring. Another is that nipples of all genders are erogenous zones with hundreds of nerve endings. They are sensitive to touch and therefore, a sexual zone by nature.

During the 2004 Super Bowl halftime show, Justin Timberlake yanked off part of Janet Jackson's costume, revealing one of her breasts. YouTube, Facebook and Twitter didn't exist yet, but the internet quickly reacted. The issue at stake? The showing of the nipple. The case, nicknamed Nipplegate (after the 1972–1974 Watergate political scandal that led to the resignation of US president Richard Nixon), received so much negative attention that Jackson and Timberlake were forced to publicly apologize.

Twelve years later, Instagram decided to censor dozens of images showing female nipples. Several celebrities, including

In our society, female breasts are sexualized.

"Cover up that bosom, which I can't endure to look on!"

—from Molière's comedy *Tartuffe, or The Impostor*

Miley Cyrus and Rihanna, then joined a #FreeTheNipple campaign, launched by actor and activist Lina Esco, that pointed out the double standard between men and women.

The hashtags #GenderlessNipples and #ManNipples were used to show that while our society commands that females' nipples be hidden, males' are freely shown.

The Genderless Nipples Instagram account shows closeups of nipples that make it difficult to identify anyone's gender. Even the social network's software algorithms no longer know how to classify them.

Bulimia

Noun, from Greek *boulimia*, "an ox's hunger"

According to the National Eating Disorder Information Centre (NEDIC), bulimia is an illness characterized by "periods of food restriction followed by binge eating, with recurrent compensating behaviours to 'purge' the body of the food." Like **anorexia**, bulimia has serious consequences on a person's body image and sexuality.

Since body dissatisfaction is often linked to low self-esteem, a person suffering from bulimia may have difficulty experiencing physical intimacy with another person. Overcoming the fear of showing your naked body to someone isn't easy if you feel deeply dissatisfied with your physical appearance and see yourself as undesirable. Talking about body image with a trusted person—a parent, friend, family member, etc.—may help you better understand the situation.

In Canada, NEDIC has a helpline that lets you talk to someone free of judgment. See nedic.ca/contact/. In the United States, the National Eating Disorders Association (NEDA) has a helpline as well as a chat feature on their website. See nationaleatingdisorders.org/contact-us.

Buttocks

Noun, from Old English *buttuc*, "short piece," from *butte*, "thick end"

Buttocks fascinate...and always have! Because all parts of the body are somewhat connected to trends and fashion, buttocks are too. The present trend encourages wide and plump posteriors like those of celebrities Nicki Minaj, Cardi B and Kim Kardashian, who have reportedly undergone plastic surgery to achieve these shapes. But buttocks can be found in all shapes and sizes: big, small, wide, narrow, plump, flat...! There's no model to follow and certainly no instruction manual for buttocks.

A THOUSAND AND ONE BUMS

Since 2015, Montreal artists Frédérique Marseille and Émilie Mercier have been photographing buttocks. Their project *1001 fesses* ("1,001 buttocks") shows the diversity of female bodies. The origins and ages of the models don't matter. The idea is for viewers to love themselves a little more and to appreciate all bodies, regardless of age, size and shape. See 1001fessesproject.com.

CERVICAL MUCUS
CISGENDER
CLIMAX
CLITORIS
COMMUNICATION
CONDOM
CONSENT
CONTRACEPTION
CUNNILINGUS
CYBERBULLYING

C

Cervical Mucus

Cervical: adjective, from Latin *cervicalis*, "of the neck or cervix"
Mucus: noun, from Latin *mucus*, "secretion"

Cervical mucus is a kind of mucus (similar to what comes out of your nose) secreted by glands in and around the cervix. It varies in texture, color and amount during the **menstrual cycle** (see entry), especially around ovulation, and thus provides information about most fertile period of people with a female reproductive system. At the beginning of the cycle, menstrual blood mixes with cervical mucus. Then there's a "drier" period during which the mucus is much less abundant. It later becomes thick, sticky and opaque. Finally—and this is the sign of the fertile period—cervical mucus becomes transparent and elastic, much like egg white.

Even if you observe your cervical mucus very closely to calculate fertile and infertile times, avoiding sex around the time of ovulation, you really have to know your body well to rely fully on this method of contraception. To be on the safe side, combine this method with another, such as

Looking at your cervical mucus to calculate fertile and infertile times is one contraceptive method. But experts recommend that you combine this method with another to increase effectiveness.

the Knaus–Ogino method, the symptothermal method or the pelvic examination (in which you feel the position of the cervix with two fingers...yep!). (See **contraception**.)

Remember, however, that there's always a risk of pregnancy, even when using these methods, and the most reliable way to avoid an **unwanted pregnancy** is to use a condom in addition to another contraceptive method.

TRACK YOUR CERVICAL MUCUS

CYCLE PERIOD (varies between individuals)	CONSISTENCY	FERTILITY
Between days 1 and 5	Mixed with the period, therefore not very apparent	No
Between days 5 and 10	Dry	No
Between days 10 and 12	Thick, sticky and opaque	Yes
Between days 12 and 14	Transparent, elastic (like egg white)	Yes
Between days 14 and 18	Thick, viscous and not very abundant	Yes
Between day 18 and the end of the cycle	Dry	Yes

Cisgender

Adjective, from Latin *cis*, "on this side of," and English *gender*, from Middle French *gendre*, "kind, type"

....

A person is described as cisgender when they are born with a sex that matches their gender **identity**—for example, a person who was born with a vagina and identifies as "female." Cisgender is therefore the opposite of *transgender* (see **transgender (person)**), which describes someone born with a sex that doesn't match their gender identity.

In the same semantic family, we find:

Cisnormativity

This is the false idea that all people are naturally cisgender and that being cisgender is the norm. In this system of thought, people who don't meet this definition—trans people, for example—are considered nonstandard.

Cissexism

In our cisnormative Western society, which considers being cisgender the norm, people who aren't cisgender are often discriminated against. This type of discrimination is called cissexism.

Cisgender is the opposite of transgender.

Climax

Noun and verb, from Latin *climax*, "emphatic figure of speech"

....

Climax is the final stage of sexual **arousal** and is the release of an intense tension in the body. It can happen when you masturbate or when you're being masturbated by your partner, when you receive oral sex, during a vaginal or anal penetration...it can even happen without touching or being touched, such as while you're sleeping and dreaming, or when you're in a certain state of mind that causes you to reach a high-enough state of sexual excitement.

Climaxing doesn't have to be the ultimate goal of sex.

Some say they've climaxed while sleeping, others while exerting pressure on their penis by squeezing their thighs, and others by simply seeing their partner having an orgasm.

But climaxing doesn't have to be the ultimate goal of a sexual experience, whether you're alone or in company. It can be very enjoyable and satisfying to give yourself pleasure without systematically reaching orgasm.

Recent studies show that 95 percent of heterosexual men have orgasms most of the time during sex, followed closely by gay men (89 percent). Heterosexual women are the least likely to have an orgasm during sex (only 65 percent do), along with bisexual women (66 percent). Lesbian women experience orgasm 86 percent of the time. These numbers confirm the falseness of the well-known equation "orgasm = penis + vagina"!

A DOSE OF HAPPINESS

When you're climaxing, the brain sends hormones such as dopamine and serotonin into your body. It's like being injected with a large dose of happiness. That's why climaxing can feel so extraordinary!

Reaching climax and having orgasms can help you:

> relax;
> have fun;
> sleep better;
> relieve menstrual pain.

Clitoris

Noun, New Latin from Greek *kleitoris*

....

The clitoris is the outcast among the family of female private parts. And yet it's the only organ in the body that's used exclusively for **pleasure**. Cool, right? Quite an extraordinary organ! Only recently have people started to talk openly about this part of the female body, which is much bigger than many people think. What was for a long time believed to be a tiny bit of flesh can in fact be 4 to 6 inches (10 to 15 centimeters) long!

Part of the clitoris, called the glans, is external, and the rest is hidden inside the body, just behind the vulva. Only a few provinces in Canada list the clitoris in educational materials about female genitalia.

Female sex is typically described as either a clitoral or a vaginal experience. But this simplistic division is incorrect. Sexual pleasure for the female body can be experienced on many levels. Many women will potentially feel pleasure through clitoral stimulation when the branches of their clitoris are stimulated inside the **vagina**. The G-spot is thought to be a portion of the internal clitoris and can be another erogenous zone for women. It's therefore not penetration in itself that generates an orgasm, but rather the stroking, touching and stimulating of the clitoris.

So, clitoral or vaginal? It is most often the *clitoris* that's responsible for women's sexual pleasure.

READ

The Vagina Bible: The Vulva and the Vagina—Separating the Myth from the Medicine by Dr. Jen Gunter (2019).

THE CLITORIS ACCORDING TO LORI MALÉPART-TRAVERSY

Lori Malépart-Traversy directed *Le clitoris*, an animated short film that has toured the world and won numerous awards. And for good reason: it's funny and well-crafted and explains clearly, in less than four minutes, why people have put aside this part of the body for too long and why the clitoris deserves to be celebrated.

The G-spot

The famous G-spot! Time and time again you see mainstream magazines touting tips and tricks for locating this elusive and mysterious part of the female genital anatomy. It's usually described as a specific area inside the vagina that when stimulated results in an orgasm every time. Unfortunately, there seems to be little scientific evidence to conclude that the G-spot actually exists. But it is well known that the two legs of the **clitoris** that run along the inside of your body can reach up to 6 inches (15 centimeters) in length. The current assumption is that the G-spot could be an area where the clitoris is rubbed during intercourse via the vagina. This friction could facilitate orgasm.

But remember that sexual pleasure, including orgasm, is usually the product of a combination of elements—sexual arousal, adequate stimulation, body and mind relaxation, comfort, desire, etc.—that allow you to let go and, perhaps, **climax**. G-spot or G-"zone"—it doesn't matter. The main thing is to have fun!

TRAVELING CLITORISES

To demystify the clitoris, artist Laura Kingsley started drawing clitorises in public spaces with chalks. She's taken her project from Washington, DC, to San Francisco, from London to New Orleans. Follow her on Instagram @clitorosity.

Communication

Noun, from Old French *comunicacion*, "act of discussing, debating, conferring"

While sexuality always starts with **consent**, it's communication that keeps it healthy.

Knowing how to express your needs, desires and limits is essential to achieve a fulfilling sex life. It's extremely important to be able to say what you like and don't like, what you wish to explore, what arouses you and what doesn't, what inspires or repels you, what you think and feel. All social interactions, whether they be between family members, friends, lovers or sexual partners, take place through communication. The best communication requires good listening skills, openness, empathy and and a desire to keep all exchanges fair and respectful.

Condom

Noun, perhaps from Latin *condere*, "to hide," or Italian *guanto*, "a glove"

Many people choose not to use a condom when having sex, for various reasons: condoms can reduce sensations during penetration and restrain the erection; they smell of latex and can leave an odor on the penis; some people develop a latex allergy; they're not free; they're an obstacle to spontaneity and must be nearby when the opportunity for sex arises. *However*, condoms remain the most effective protection against **STDs** or **STIs**.

Condoms are also an excellent, affordable and accessible method of contraception. The decision to put on a condom is about taking responsibility for your sexual health and the sexual health of your partners. It's about avoiding anxiety and stress if you don't know too much about your partner's sexual past.

> Condoms are the most effective protection against STDs or STIs.

The person or people you want to have sex with may refuse to use a condom. A few things to remember if or when that situation arises:

> Without a condom, sex is more stressful, especially if you're not sure whether you or your partners have an STD or STI. Wearing a condom takes that stress away and allows you to focus on what counts — pleasure!

> The pullout method is proven to be unsafe. Condoms can prevent unwanted pregnancies.

> If you or your partner find that putting on the condom breaks the spontaneity of sex and affects your arousal levels a bit, remember that penetration isn't the only pleasurable move. There are lots of other gestures and caresses, and exciting areas can be explored with your hands, fingers or tongue. If condoms start feeling like barriers to sex, use them as a driver of change and exploration by including them in your foreplay.

MALE OR FEMALE?

	WHAT ARE THEY?	PROS AND CONS
MALE (EXTERNAL) **CONDOMS**	They're like transparent, cylindrical "balloons," most often made of latex,* and they unroll around the penis, leaving a small space above the glans to collect semen and secretions. During sex, the latex prevents direct contact between the penis and the vagina, anus or mouth, and acts as a protection. When the person wearing the condom ejaculates, their semen remains in the condom.	Condoms protect against STDs or STIs, aren't expensive and can be obtained everywhere (in pharmacies, convenience stores, school infirmaries, clinics, school vending machines, etc.). Some healthcare centers or youth agencies provide free condoms. They can decrease sensation during sex. Using a condom takes a little practice—you have to remove it from its packaging without tearing it and unroll it over the penis in the right direction so that the condom stays in place. Practicing together can be fun.
FEMALE (INTERNAL) **CONDOMS**	They're transparent latex tubes with a ring on each end. You insert the first ring in the back of the vagina and place the second over the vulva. The penis can then enter the vagina, covered with the plastic envelope that prevents direct contact.	Female condoms also protect from STDs or STIs and are an effective method of contraception. They can make noise and slip inside the vagina during sex. They're a little more expensive, though they can be ordered at the pharmacy or on the internet.

* Some people are allergic to latex. Latex-free condoms are available in pharmacies.

Consent

Noun and verb, from Old French verb *consentir*, "to allow, grant permission," from Latin *consentire*, "to agree"

This is where it all starts! To consent means to actively and freely agree to sexual activities with someone. Consent isn't a half yes or a hesitant yes. It's an enthusiastic, authentic and sincere yes. It's also a yes that can become a no if you change your mind later on.

According to the American Sexual Health Association, "Consent is an agreement that is willfully given without any external pressure or factors. In order for someone to consent to sexual activity, participants must continuously communicate before, during and after sexual activity—this is the only way to establish clear boundaries between participants and allows for a relaxing experience."

It's that simple. Without a yes, it's a no (see **#MeToo**).

The age of consent is the age at which a person is considered in law to be able to consent to sexual activity. Someone above this age who has sex with someone below it can often be charged with statutory rape, even if the younger person wants to consent.

HIT OR MISS?

Is there consent if...

1. I want to have sex with my partner, who's drunk a lot of alcohol but also seems interested. I feel like this is okay.

   Answer: No. The word to highlight here is *seems*. Do you know what that person really wants? When alcohol or other drugs are involved, consent is canceled, since the person doesn't have all of their faculties and is incapable of making an informed decision.

2. My partner wants to explore anal sex. It piques my curiosity. I'm a little scared, but I feel like I can trust them and that it'll be okay. Besides, I want to.

   Answer: Yes. So glad to hear you feel you trust this person. Give it a try and know that you can always change your mind in the process. You may have fears (justified, as this is brand-new to you), but you're okay with exploring this facet of your sexuality and feel safe and secure.

3. I meet someone at a party. We talk. There's chemistry. I feel there's a strong attraction between us. We kiss, and they offer to end the evening at their place. I decide to go with them, because I really want to have sex with them. Once home, we exchange caresses, kiss and end up in bed. While earlier at the party I had a very strong urge to have sex with this person, I now think that this moment alone with them made me happy—I don't wish to push things further and would rather go home. When I tell them that, they reply, "You came here because you wanted to, so now you have to go all the way!" I feel bad for having changed my mind and tell myself they're not wrong. I *did* initiate the move, so I go to bed with them, even though I would prefer to leave.

Answer: No. If you change your mind along the way, don't feel comfortable and want to end a sexual relationship, you can withdraw your consent at any time. Consent isn't set in stone. Anyone can make it known to the other, at their convenience and regardless of the situation, that they no longer wish to participate. And your partner has to respect that.

4. Someone I have been seeing recently tells me they don't feel comfortable with receiving oral sex. I tell myself they have never dealt with an expert like me, and I do it anyway, despite their reluctance.

Answer: No. Your partner is uncomfortable, and even if you consider yourself an amazing lover, it won't change that fact. They have informed you of their discomfort, so just abstain from oral sex and focus on other things that feels good for the both of you.

ALCOHOL

Alcohol has a disinhibiting effect, meaning it relaxes our bodies. Scientists believe—although there isn't consensus—that the alcohol molecule (ethanol) enters the bloodstream and slows down the normal processes of neurons, which are the cells that transmit information to the brain. Alcohol makes you less alert and causes the body to secrete dopamine, an addictive substance that makes you euphoric (excited and happy). As a result, you're not in your normal state after drinking alcohol, and therefore you cannot make rational, sensible decisions.

Alcohol has the effect of encouraging people to do things that in another context they wouldn't do for fear of embarrassing themselves, creating stress or appearing irrational.

When a person is under the influence of alcohol or drugs, they cannot give their informed consent, and consent is essential for any sexual activity to take place. Without it, you are committing sexual assault.

When a person is under the influence of alcohol, they cannot give their informed consent.

In 2016, according to Statistics Canada, 19 percent of Canadians 12 and over (roughly 5.8 million people) reported abusing alcohol.

In Canada, Kids Help Phone has online resources as well as a toll-free phone line to support teens seeking help for substance abuse.

1-800-668-6868

kidshelpphone.ca/topic/emotional-well-being/substance-use

Contraception

Noun, from the Latin prefix *contra-* , "against," and *conception*, from Old French *concepcion*, "conceive in the womb"

....

Contraception is intentional prevention of pregnancy. Methods of contraception, called contraceptive methods, are ways to avoid getting pregnant. Anyone who has an active sex life and wants to avoid an **unwanted pregnancy** needs to know about the various contraceptive methods available. However, no method is 100 percent effective.

Condoms, for example, protect against **STDs** or **STIs**. Some contraceptive methods, such as the birth control pill, regulate the menstrual cycle or even reduce premenstrual symptoms and cramps.

There are four categories of contraceptive methods.

Barrier methods

Contraceptives in this category create a physical barrier that prevents sperm from entering the uterus to fertilize the egg. Female and male condoms (see **condom**), diaphragms, spermicides, cervical caps (such as Lea's Shield) and hormone-free intra-uterine devices (IUDs) are examples of barrier methods. Only condoms also protect against STDs or STIs.

Hormonal methods

Hormonal methods use chemical processes to prevent ovulation (see **menstrual cycle**). They therefore have an effect on the body, known as a systemic effect, because the entire system is affected. This category includes, among others, oral contraceptives, vaginal rings, contraceptive patches, contraceptive injections, such as Depo-Provera, and hormonal IUDs. Very important: hormonal methods do not protect against STDs or STIs.

Natural methods

Natural methods don't involve the ingestion of any chemicals and have no systemic effect on the body. Most rely on women calculating the fertile and infertile periods of their cycle, such as "calendar" or Knaus–Ogino method, the symptothermal method and cervical mucus monitoring (see **cervical mucus**). Other natural methods are withdrawal or interrupted coitus, and abstinence. Apart from abstinence, these methods do not protect against STDs or STIs. Several natural contraceptive methods can be combined with another. For example, the calendar method can be combined with cervical mucus monitoring. These methods are not recommended for adolescents, for several reasons:

> A teenager's menstrual cycle may not yet be completely stabilized and could vary, making it impossible to calculate the period of ovulation (or fertility) accurately and reliably.

> Natural contraceptive methods require an excellent knowledge of your body, which is difficult in adolescence, a period of major physical changes and transformations and different emotional states.

> Natural methods require regular and precise monitoring, which hardly fits with the schedule and rhythm of many teenagers, who often have busy social lives and variable sleep habits.

Irreversible methods (or sterilization)

As their name suggests, these methods of contraception are permanent and irreversible without surgery. They may be suitable for people who have decided not to have more children or any children at all. These methods are not recommended for teens and young adults because it's a bit soon for you to decide whether are not you'll want to have children in the future. These methods do not protect against STDs or STIs.

Tubal ligation

In this surgery the fallopian tubes are blocked or cut, preventing the egg from traveling to the uterus and being fertilized by a sperm.

Vasectomy

This surgical procedure involves blocking or cutting the vas deferens tubes to keep sperm out of the semen. Erections are still possible afterward, but the semen no longer contains any sperm.

To learn more about contraceptive methods, visit the Planned Parenthood website, plannedparenthood.org.

YOUR FIRST TRIP TO THE GYNECOLOGIST

The first few conversations about contraception can be a bit awkward and uncomfortable. That's normal. It's a new world. During an appointment with a gynecologist, there's a lot to talk about, and you may also have to undress for a medical or gynecological exam. You can also go to a public health nurse for information and advice.

Questions the gynecologist may ask include:

> Do you have any known health problems?

> Have you had your period?

> How's your menstrual cycle (length, pain, symptoms, bleeding flow, etc.)?

> What method do you use to manage your period (tampon, pad, menstrual cup, etc.)?

> Have you ever had sex or are you planning to have sex soon?

> If you have had sex, did you use protection such as condoms?

> Do you know the sexual past of the partner(s) with whom you had sex?

> Do you have a boyfriend, a girlfriend or a partner with whom you have sex on a regular basis, or do you have multiple partners?

> What do you know about contraception? What methods have you heard of? Do you prefer a specific method, and why? Are you anxious about certain methods?

> Do you smoke cigarettes? (Some contraceptive methods don't work for smokers.)

These questions are designed to help the gynecologist prescribe the most appropriate contraceptive method for you. Sometimes you have to test several methods before you find the right one. For example, some people are sensitive to hormonal fluctuations and will need very-low-dose oral contraceptives.

BARRIER METHODS

	HOW IT WORKS	PROS AND CONS
CONDOM	(See **condom**.)	(See **condom**.)
HORMONE-FREE INTRAUTERINE DEVICE (IUD)	This is a small device shaped like a T, the horizontal bar covered with copper. The copper changes the vagina's pH and slows the sperm traveling to the uterus, destroying them in the meantime. Copper causes inflammation of the endometrium, which prevents the uterus from receiving a fertilized egg. IUDs must be installed by a doctor or gynecologist.	Durable: Once installed, an IUD's lifespan is 5 to 10 years. Since it's inside the body and there's no manipulation to do, you can forget about it (which you can't with a pill that needs to be taken every day, for example). May lengthen periods for one to two days and increase cramping and bleeding.
SPERMICIDE	This is a chemical (often nonoxynol-9) that immobilizes and destroys sperm. Spermicide is most effective when used along with another contraceptive method, such as a cervical cap or diaphragm.	No hormonal effect on the body. Not very effective on its own; may cause odors and irritation; if applied in excessive quantity, can create small lacerations on the skin.
CERVICAL CAP	This is a silicone container that looks like a small plug and fits over the cervix. The cap can't be used alone; spermicide should be added to ensure effectiveness.	Can be used for successive sexual relations; no danger of leaving it inside the body for a long time after sex; no hormonal effect on the body. Requires a specific cap size and some practice.

	HOW IT WORKS	PROS AND CONS
DIAPHRAGM	This is a small latex or silicone disk the size of the palm of your hand, to which spermicide—a gel, foam, or cream substance that kills sperm—is added. The disk is inserted up to two hours before sexual intercourse.	Reusable; no hormonal effect on the body. Requires some practice to insert correctly and comfortably; interferes with spontaneity (you have to remember to insert it before having sexual intercourse); may be uncomfortable during sex.
LEA'S SHIELD	This is a small ringed cap that is inserted into the vagina and placed on the cervix. It is more effective if used with spermicide.	Reusable; can stay in place for 48 hours. Requires more handling; can be a bit uncomfortable during penetration.

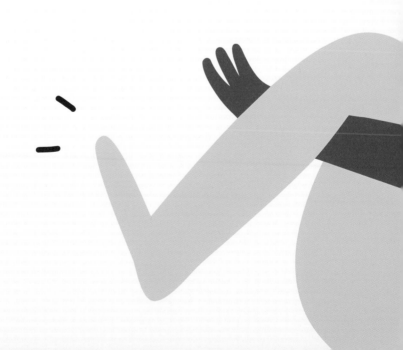

HORMONAL METHODS

	HOW IT WORKS	PROS AND CONS
HORMONAL IUD	Like the hormone-free IUD, this is shaped like a T. Because it contains hormones, it works the same way other hormonal contraceptives do, stopping ovulation and preventing implantation of the egg.	No forgetting possible, because it's placed directly inside the body and functions without human intervention; it may decrease menstrual cramps; it's very effective. Must be fitted and removed by a doctor; may cause side effects, such as heavier bleeding or longer menstrual cycle. You can always discuss potential side effects with your healthcare professional.
ORAL CONTRACEPTIVE	Also known as "the pill" and "birth control pill." Oral contraceptives work in three steps: they prevent ovulation, change the cervical mucus and change the endometrium to prevent the implantation of an egg.	Simple and effective method that involves taking one pill a day. Risk of forgetting to take the pill; must be prescribed by a doctor or public health nurse; possible side effects, such as headaches, nausea and decreased libido.
DEPO-PROVERA	This intramuscular contraceptive injection (yep, a shot in the muscle!) is given every three months. Like oral contraceptives, it works in three stages.	No risk of forgetting to use contraception; can reduce menstrual cramps. Can cause weight gain and loss of bone density, is difficult to get rid of afterward. Not typically prescribed for teenagers. Please consult your healthcare professional to discuss side effects.

	HOW IT WORKS	PROS AND CONS
CONTRACEPTIVE PATCH	It looks like a small square band-aid that is placed on the upper back, abdomen, a buttock or on the outer part of the upper arm. It works like oral contraceptives do, releasing a dose of hormones every day.	Very effective if used properly; forgetting is unlikely, because the patch is changed only once a week; possibility of requiring smaller doses of hormones, as they are absorbed through the skin. Can peel off and sometimes trigger skin reactions; can also cause side effects, such as skin irritation where it is placed and irregular menstrual bleeding.
VAGINAL RING	This small, soft plastic ring is placed in your vagina, where it releases hormones every day, acting in three stages just like oral contraceptives. It must be changed every three weeks.	Forgetfulness is unlikely since it is placed and left in for three weeks. Very effective if used properly. May cause side effects; requires an adequate knowledge of your body, because it is inserted by you.

NATURAL METHODS

	HOW IT WORKS	PROS AND CONS
CALENDAR OR KNAUS–OGINO METHOD	The period of ovulation is calculated based on the menstrual cycle. During this time partners use contraception or practice abstinence* or withdrawal.** To calculate your ovulation period, first take note of the length of your menstrual cycles over a period of 6 to 12 months. What day should you start counting? It's simple: the first day of the cycle is the first day of your period. Then note the shortest and longest cycles. Subtract 20 days from the shortest cycle. For example, if the shortest cycle is 27 days, subtract 20 from that, which equals 7. This means the seventh day of the cycle is the start of your fertile period. Then subtract 11 days (Knaus method) or 10 days (Ogino method) from the longest cycle—say, 32 days, and you get 21 days (Knaus) or 22 days (Ogino). The end of the fertile period is the 21st or 22nd day of the cycle, depending on which method you used. Your period of fertility, then, is the 7th to the 22nd day.	Natural method; no effects on the body; allows you to better understand your body and the changes that take place during your cycle. Requires daily monitoring and a little calculation; requires either another contraceptive method, withdrawal or abstinence, which can be frustrating when you want to have sex. (But never forget that there are a thousand and one ways to have a sexual relationship with your partner(s), and penetration is just one of many.)

	HOW IT WORKS	PROS AND CONS
SYMPTOTHERMAL METHOD	Starting on the first day of your cycle (your first day of menstruation), you take your body temperature using a thermometer (oral, anal or vaginal) and record it on a chart that will allow you to monitor your cycle. You should also note the texture of your cervical mucus and the position of your cervix (lower or higher). This data determines when fertilization can take place.	Same as for the calendar method. Ideally, take a course on the symptothermal method to learn how to manage your chart—it's a little complicated—and how to properly carry out your observations of the mucus and cervix. The symptothermal method is usually recommended for people who wish to become pregnant.

* Abstinence means not having sex during the ovulation period.

** Withdrawal, in the context of a sexual relationship that includes a female person and a male person, refers to the action of withdrawing the penis from the vagina so that ejaculation occurs outside the female genitals. However, be aware that the pre-ejaculatory fluid (commonly called pre-cum) discharged from the penis when it's aroused may also contain sperm. Withdrawal is, therefore, not without risk.

Cunnilingus

Noun, from Latin *cunnus*, "vulva," and *lingere*, "to lick"

Cunnilingus is one of the oral sex practices. It's more commonly known as "eating out," "eat a peach" or "go down on." It's stimulation done with the mouth and tongue on the vulva and clitoris. It's never an obligation to give cunnilingus (or receive it)—you give or receive cunnilingus when you want to please your partner and feel sexual pleasure yourself. It can be very enjoyable. As with anal sex or **fellatio**, there isn't a unique technique or set of instructions—you just have to make sure you're comfortable, communicate what you like and don't like, open up to your partner in order to better understand their body and their desires, and try new things.

To avoid contracting **STDs** or **STIs**, a **dental dam** can be used during cunnilingus.

Cyberbullying

Noun, from the prefix of Greek origin *cyber-*, "relating to the internet or virtual reality," and the verb *to bully*, from the noun *bully*, probably from Middle Dutch *boel(e)*, "brother; lover"

Cyberbullying, or cyberharassment, is using information technologies (smartphones, social networks, computers, etc.) to harass or intimidate someone. Examples include writing hateful or degrading comments on Instagram under a selfie of someone in your class, sending mean or threatening texts or, worse, uploading a video on YouTube showing a classmate in an embarrassing situation to publicly ridicule them.

Cyberbullying isn't just unacceptable but can also be illegal and punishable by law, depending on the seriousness of the actions or words. The police can be called in, and a court case could follow. The perpetrator may be ordered to appear before a judge and even end up in jail.

Obviously, cyberbullying can have serious affects on the person being bullied. Bullied people typically feel persecuted and so isolate themselves. They're afraid and constantly on guard. It can greatly affect their mental health and even lead some to **suicide**.

If you're a victim of cyberbullying, or if you witness cyberharassment, you should talk to adults in positions of authority (teachers, parents, etc.) who can offer help. It's important not to keep it to yourself. Speaking out about intimidation helps you and others dealing with the same problems who may not want talk about it. It's also helps make sure that schools and organizations find solutions and implement them.

BULLYING OR BEING BULLIED?

In certain situations, perhaps without even realizing it, *you* may become the bully. For example, you might want to be part of the group and end up harassing a person just to follow the herd. Giving in to this kind of social pressure is never good. When you witness bullying, you have a duty to report it, even if it isn't always easy. If you don't talk about it and report it, bullying persists and escalates over time, making it harder to find solutions. To talk about it or to find help, check out teenlineonline.org or kidshelpphone.ca.

WHAT IS REVENGE PORN?

Revenge porn can be a form of cyberbullying. It's the public sharing of explicit (sexual or erotic) material without the consent of the person involved for the purpose of personal revenge. The term *sextortion* is also used. Here's a typical example of this act. A person doesn't accept being dumped by their partner. To retaliate, they upload intimate photos and videos of their ex in order to publicly humiliate them. Revenge porn is a violent act that can have a significant and harmful impact on the victim's life.

It's also an act punishable by law. People who distribute revenge porn can face high fines and even be convicted and jailed. Canada's Criminal Code prohibits "non-consensual distribution of intimate images," and violators can be sentenced to up to five years in prison.

GO AND SEE

The YWCA Canada website has an interesting breakdown of statistics and a guide to revenge porn prosecution: ywcacanada.ca/guide-on-sexual-image-based-abuse.

DEADNAMING
DEMISEXUALITY
DENTAL DAM
DESIRE
DISABILITY
DISCRIMINATION
DIVERSITY
DRUGS

D

Deadnaming

Dead: adjective, form Old English *dead*, "having ceased to live"
Naming: noun, from Old English *namian*, "to bestow a name on"

When you're born, one of the first things you receive is a name. Your name helps define your identity and, in most cases, will follow you throughout your life. For some people, however, a name is a relic of a part of their past they would rather forget. Many trans or nonbinary people change their name at some point in their lives to be more in tune with their gender **identity**. For these people, a birth name can act as a painful reminder of a previous, defunct identity. In these cases, the birth name is called a deadname, meaning an identity the person no longer uses or even overtly rejects. Just like **misgendering**, calling a person by their deadname can be a violent gesture, even when done without any intention of hurting.

Demisexuality

Noun, from the prefix of Latin origin *demi-*, "half," and from Latin *sexualis*, "concerning sex," from *sexus*, "sex, gender"

Being demisexual doesn't mean you make love *half*way or *half*-heartedly. Demisexuality is a sexual orientation where people don't feel sexual attraction to a person unless they have an emotional bond with them.

Demisexual people aren't capable of having a **one-night stand** with a partner.

The prefix *demi-* isn't pejorative—it doesn't mean "incomplete" but simply that this type of sexuality is located halfway between sexuality and asexuality. Demisexuality is also associated with **gray (a)sexuality**.

Dental Dam

Dental: adjective, from Latin *dentalis*, "concerning
the teeth," from *dens*, "tooth"
Dam: noun, from Middle English *dam*

Although it's a little-known fact, dental dams are sometimes used for oral sex, such as **fellatio**, **cunnilingus** and anilingus (one of the anal sex practices). Used by dentists to isolate the teeth being worked on from the rest of the patient's mouth, thereby preventing infection, these small latex membranes have been adapted from their original function and added to the (short) list of protections against **STDs** or **STIs**. Using dental dams is simple. Place the small square membrane, which looks like a thin sheet of paper, on the **vulva**, **penis** or anus and stroke these parts of the body through the membrane. That way you'll avoid direct contact with your partner's bodily fluids and possible lesions...and go on with the fun!

Desire

Noun, from Old French *desir*, "a coveting"; verb, from Old French *desirer*, "to covet." Both from Latin *desiderare*, "to want, long for"

To feel desire is to wish for something or someone in particular. For example, you might desire a really cool hat that you saw in the store. That sort of desire is oriented toward an object, and it obviously doesn't have the same meaning as when you sexually desire someone. In that case, we're talking about a **physical and sexual attraction**—which can also be emotional—toward a person. You can also desire a specific sexual or romantic gesture, such as a kiss, a hug, a penetration, rubbing or a touch, etc.

When you feel desire for someone, it's more of an impulse than a rational decision. So you have to listen to yourself to understand what interests you sexually. Desire can teach you a lot about your attractions, your preferences. Do you feel desire for a specific person? People who identify as male or female? Gender-nonconforming people? There is no right or wrong answer, especially since desire can fluctuate throughout our lives.

> "What one does not have, and what one is not, and what one lacks... such are the objects of desire and love."
>
> —Plato, *Symposium*, section 200e

It's important to realize that desire is experienced internally first. You may have a lot of fun imagining an erotic scenario with someone you like, for example, but decide to stop there. You may have felt in that instance that thinking about it was enough and you don't feel the need to go further. And that's totally **normal**. It's part of what's called fantasizing.

Disability

Noun, from Latin origin *dis-*, "negation, incompleteness, reversal, removal" + the adjective *able* (from Old French *hable*, "handy," from Latin *habilis*, "handy")

Sex is for everyone, and that includes people with physical disabilities.* Contrary to what many people still think, people with disabilities aren't devoid of sexual desire. On the contrary! While sexual activities are likely to be different for people with disabilities—physical sensations as well—and may require adjustments, the fact remains that they need intimacy and/or sex with their partners, just like everyone else.

A 2017 survey found that one in five (22 percent) people in Canada over the age of 15 lived with one or more disabilities.

* The situation may be different for people with intellectual disabilities because they need to be able to give their consent to sexual interactions, which may not be possible in some cases.

WATCH

The Netflix TV show *Special* explores the sexuality of people living with disabilities through the experience of a young gay man with cerebral palsy.

Our society caters to "ableism" or "ableist privilege," meaning that most things are built and organized for "valid and capable" bodies, according to certain standards that ignore the needs and realities of a part of the population living with one or more disabilities.

Discrimination

Noun, from Latin *discriminatio*, "separation"

Discrimination is the act of deciding, doing or saying something that isolates and bullies a person on the basis of their individual characteristics, such as their race, body, sexual orientation, gender expression or sexual identity. Depending on the form it takes, discrimination may be illegal and punishable by law, such as when a person is denied a job because of their **sexual orientation**.

Discrimination can take place in any environment, at school, at work or at home. It renders people vulnerable and has a huge impact on their self-esteem, body perception, sexual health and overall health. There are ways to fight discrimination, including through the Canadian Human Rights Commission or the Civil Rights Division in the United States.

BEHAVIORS
NEEDING CHANGE

Several types of discrimination aren't illegal but cause deep and systemic problems in society. Think about:

> women who receive a smaller salary than men doing the same work;

> trans people excluded from social activities in their workplace because their colleagues and bosses are uncomfortable around them;

> homosexual couples who are refused entry into bars;

> boys who are told they will never become "real men" by a parent who finds them too "effeminate."

Diversity

Noun, from Old French *diversite*, "diversity," from
Latin *diversitas*, "diversity, difference"

Any representation of society as a whole must include diversity—body diversity, sexual and gender diversity and cultural diversity.

Body diversity

Body diversity means representing all body types, especially in the media, and moving away from beauty standards that are often unattainable and don't correspond to the vast majority of people. The desire to see different bodies represented has become a hot social issue, to such an extent that some brands are riding the wave of the body-positive movement, selecting models of different sizes in their advertisements. We're also seeing more and more ads featuring beauty products used by people with different skin types, such as those who proudly display their vitiligo (a skin condition that discolors the epidermis and creates white spots). There's still work to be done, of course, but things are slowly progressing.

Diversity's inclusive and representative qualities can have a significant positive impact on the lives of young people.

Sexual and gender diversity

Sexual and gender diversity is the adequate representation of sexual orientations other than heterosexuality and of gender identities that do not conform to the **cisgender** "norm"—**transgender**, **queer** and **nonbinary**.

The initialism **LGBTQQIP2SAA+** (see definition) is often used to refer to sexual minorities.

Cultural diversity

Cultural diversity is the adequate representation of members of different cultural backgrounds, such as Black, Indigenous and People of Color, among many others.

When making the effort and taking the time to build a realistic and inclusive representation of the world with cultural sensitivity, we show respect for people who are part of minority groups and challenge systemic racism.

Drugs

Noun, from Old French *droge*, "medication, cure"

....

"Sex, drugs and rock 'n' roll…" This cult slogan right out of the 1970s has been reused in every imaginable way, in particular to describe parties (or entire lives!) consumed by hot encounters, loud music and different illicit substances.

There's probably a real scientific link between sex, drugs and rock 'n' roll. According to a recent study by researchers at McGill University in Montreal, "the chemical mechanisms of the brain underlying sexual pleasure or the pleasure elicited by the use of recreational drugs or food also play a determining role in musical pleasure." Not a surprise that people can become addicted to one or the other—our brains are being manipulated!

The reality is that sometimes you can be tempted to try certain drugs. Because it's intriguing, because you want to follow your friends, because it's exciting to "live a little dangerously." In fact, wanting to take drugs is just as normal as wanting to avoid them. The fact remains that drug consumption carries great risks for your physical and mental health. Drugs and **alcohol** can have disinhibiting effects on behavior and lead people to act recklessly or make uninformed decisions. When you're intoxicated, you're unable to give your true **consent** to a sexual act. There's also a greater risk of not using protection, such as condoms, during sex.

CANNABIS AND YOU

As of October 17, 2018, the consumption of cannabis (pot) is legal in Canada. In the United States, using and possessing cannabis is illegal at the federal level but has been legalized for recreational use in 17 states and for medical use in 36 states. Although in theory the drug remains illegal for minors, some still consume it. According to a Centers for Disease Control and Prevention study on drug and cannabis use, almost 38 percent of American high school students report having used marijuana.

EJACULATION
ENDOMETRIOSIS
ERECTION
EROGENOUS ZONES
EXPLORATION

E

Ejaculation

Noun, from Middle French *éjaculation*, from Latin *ejaculari*, "to shoot out"

Simply put, ejaculation is the emission of **semen** from the **penis**. The very first ejaculation in a boy's life is called *thorarche*, and it usually happens around the age of 12 or 13. But it can happen later than this, which isn't a problem. It occurs most of the time unconsciously, during the night, after a particularly inspiring (read erotic, sexual) dream. This type of ejaculation is called a nocturnal emission or nocturnal penile tumescence, but it's known informally as a wet dream. It's completely normal and natural. Wet dreams also occur in adulthood, although more rarely.

The ejaculation that occurs after masturbation or sexual intercourse works like this: when sexual arousal increases in intensity (through touching, being touched or penetration), the semen leaves the testicles and goes into the urethra, and then it is expelled from the penis—like a jet of water—by contractions generated at the time of orgasm.

When you're young, controlling your urges or desires is hard, you get aroused quickly and can ejaculate earlier than intended

> The amount of ejaculated semen varies between a half and three-quarters of a teaspoon!

during sex. One way to deal with this is to relax and take the time to build up the excitement more slowly. However, if the symptom persists, you can consult a doctor or a specialist (urologist) to discuss it and try to find the cause.

Women also ejaculate. Just like with male ejaculation, female ejaculation happens when fluid is expelled during orgasm. Particularly heavy ejaculation in women is sometimes referred to as "squirting" (see **lubrication**). However, with most women, ejaculation is too discreet to be noticed.

Endometriosis

Noun, from the prefix of Greek origin *endo-*, "within," Greek *mētra*, "womb"

Difficult to diagnose, endometriosis is a gynecological disease that affects 10 to 15 percent of women of childbearing age, according to the US National Library of Medicine.

Endometriosis is associated with infertility (the inability to get pregnant).

Endometriosis is a chronic disorder, which means it is a long-term condition. It occurs when the endometrium, which is the tissue that lines the inner wall of the **uterus** and thickens in preparation for possible pregnancy, "escapes" from its territory and grows in other places, such as on the ovaries, the bladder and sometimes even the kidneys. When you're not pregnant, part of the lining of the uterus comes off and is expelled during your period. But when you have endometriosis, that tissue doesn't come out, which causes pain. And it can get worse—endometriosis is associated with infertility (the inability to get pregnant).

LENA DUNHAM'S
TESTIMONY

Lena Dunham, creator and star of the popular TV series *Girls*, suffered from endometriosis for a long time. In fall 2017, after years of pain and unsuccessful attempts to relieve it, she decided to have her uterus removed, a procedure called a hysterectomy.* She recounted in several interviews the complex (and painful) journey she had to endure before she finally had her uterus removed. The surgery is invasive and can't be reversed, and it means you will never be able to give birth. In an essay Dunham writes, "I know that a hysterectomy isn't the right choice for everyone, that it's not a guarantee that this pain will disappear, and that you are performing it due to your deeply held, essential and—to my mind—feminist belief that women should be able to make a choice about how they want to spend their childbearing years."

* Not all women who suffer from endometriosis need to have their uterus removed. Each case is unique and requires special treatment.

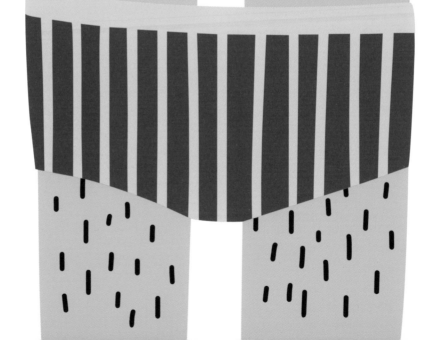

Erection

Noun, from Latin *erectio*, "process of erection," from *erigere*, "to raise; arouse"

When a touch, image or thought arouses a person with a **penis**, the brain receives a signal and sends a message through the spinal cord to send blood to the penis, which then becomes engorged with blood and hardens to form an erection. This is a simplified explanation of what happens in the body, because the process of sexual **arousal** leading to the erection is complex—it's hard-core neurophysiology (the study of the functions of the nervous system).

You can be aroused by many things. It may be something you see, like an inspiring picture or a movie scene. It may be something you do and enjoy, like working out. It may be a touch, like a hug or a kiss. Thoughts of a sexual or erotic nature may go through your head. There are lots of causes of arousal.

And by the way, when the penis is erect, you don't need to worry about urinating, because the channel that carries urine (the urethra) to the penis closes.

THE CLITORIS TOO!

When people think of an erection, they automatically think of the penis. But it's not the only organ capable of being erect. The clitoris is too! It can become hard, and its internal bulbs, which are hidden behind the vulva and can measure up to 6 inches (15 centimeters), will swell like the penis does (see **clitoris**).

HARD TO BEAT

Pornographic movies (see **pornography**) present viewers with monumental erections that last for hours and actors who ejaculate on demand. But that's not reality—everything is staged.

Male porn actors are selected for their physique and the size of their penis. They may also use medication designed to increase blood flow to the penis, such as Cialis (like Viagra but lasts longer). It's not without risk, as an erection that lasts too long can cause permanent damage.

According to a study of 500 heterosexual couples who timed each other during sex, the average erection lasts for 5.4 minutes. An erection that naturally lasts for hours and hours? Nope, not really a thing.

Erogenous Zones

Erogenous: adjective, from Greek *erōs*, "sexual love" + -*genous*, "producing"
Zone: noun, from Latin *zona*, "belt"

Erogenous zones are the areas of the body that are sexually aroused when they are stimulated by touch. They are can be specific parts of the body—the genitals, breasts, buttocks, thighs or anus.

But almost the whole body can be erogenous! In a 2016 Finnish study, some 700 participants were asked to color on pictures of naked people the parts of the body that aroused them the most during specific activities (masturbation and sex, for example). Well, it turns out that almost the whole body can be part of the sexual experience!

Exploration

Noun, from Middle French *exploration*, "process of exploring," from Latin *exploratio*, "exploration"

You can view sexuality as being above all a type of exploration—the exploration of your body, sure, but also of your desires and preferences. **Adolescence** is the time in life when you start to feel differently about other people, regardless of their gender. You wish to get closer to and more intimate with certain people. You find some people more beautiful, more attractive, than others. Your friendships are tinged with possible attractions. You forge special bonds.

By exploring and allowing yourself the freedom to be who you are, through trials and errors, you start answering important questions about your **sexual orientation** and preferences, and your gender **identity** and expression. Exploration informs you of what you like and don't like.

FALLOPIAN TUBES
FAMILY
FAT TALK
FATPHOBIA
FELLATIO
FEMININITY
FERTILITY
FIRST TIME(S)
FOREPLAY
FREE INSTINCTIVE FLOW
FRIEND WITH BENEFITS
FRIENDSHIP

Fallopian Tubes

Fallopian: adjective, from *Fallopius*, Latinized form of the
name *Gabriello Fallopio*, 16th-century Italian anatomist
and priest who first described the organ
Tube: noun, from Middle French *tube*, "tube," from Latin *tubus*, "pipe"

The fallopian tubes, also called uterine tubes and salpinges, are slender tubes that look like little arms with hands, emerging from the uterus and connecting it with the ovaries. Eggs pass from the ovaries through these tubes to the **uterus**. Each side of the uterus has one **ovary** and one fallopian tube. Sperm pass by the fallopian tubes after ejaculation in the **vagina** during hetero-sexual intercourse.

Family

Noun, from Latin *familia*, "household servants; family members"

If you're a teenager, you might sometimes find your family tiring and overwhelming. Teenagers want to be free, to explore, to have time for themselves. And your room becomes a shelter, a refuge to escape your parents' questions or comments—despite the love you feel for them.

But don't forget that family members, provided they aren't dysfunctional (for example, violent, substance abusers, etc.), play a primary role in someone's **adolescence**, a period when everything is a little uncertain and where a lot of questions arise.

For trans and gay youth, who often experience violence, harassment and oppression on a daily basis, parental support is vital. Family support has been shown to significantly decrease the risk of attempted **suicide** and depression among these youth.

Whether you're dealing with major issues or living through the most mundane of adolescences, your family should ideally provide a safe environment. You should feel supported, understood and encouraged. And if this isn't the case, surrogate families (chosen families) can be created, with people—friends, teachers, distant family members—who support you and listen to you without judgment. These trustworthy people will be there no matter what.

Fat Talk

Fat: adjective, from Old English *fætt*, "well fed; plump"
Talk: noun, from Old English *tealcian*, "to talk"

Fat talk means talking about the body in a negative way—a belly that's too soft, thighs that are too big, buttocks that are too large, a body weight that's too heavy...all physical traits are perceived negatively.

It's mostly teenage girls who engage in fat talk. For some, it becomes an almost obsessive topic of conversation. Fat talk has a negative impact on young girls' self-image and self-esteem. **Muscle talk** is the equivalent for boys.

Fatphobia

From the adjective *fat* (from Old English *fǣtt*, "well fed; plump")
and combining form -*phobia* (from Greek *phobos*, "fear")

....

Fatphobia is an abnormal and irrational fear of being fat or being around fat people. Someone who is fatphobic is hostile toward people they perceive as being fat or overweight. Fatphobia takes different forms, including *fat-shaming*, which means discriminating against, insulting or abusing a person because of their weight. It manifests in all kinds of subtle and not-so-subtle ways. People show fatphobia when they:

> make an unsolicited comment about an overweight person's food choices;

> believe that all overweight people aren't very active and don't play sports;

> say that it's overweight people's own fault that they are overweight;

> refuse healthcare to an overweight person and believe that their health problems are directly related to their weight;

> desexualize and de-eroticize the bodies of overweight people, assuming their bodies won't be attractive to other people.

This last point is especially important, as what's portrayed on television and in the movies implies that only thin people have great sex lives. Of course, nothing is further from the truth. People of all body types have great sex lives—sexuality has nothing to do with body weight or waist size. It's about having the desire for sex, the capacity to give consent to it and the physical ability to engage in it. If mainstream media represented reality, it would portray people of all body types as sexual beings.

Thin privilege

Thin privilege refers to the advantages of being thin in a society that glorifies and encourages thinness. It can mean anything from easily finding clothes in your size when you're out shopping, not being judged for what you choose to eat and receiving unbiased healthcare. Slimness is a privilege for people who meet this standard and a disadvantage for those who don't. The notion of thin privilege is used when characterizing the treatment of overweight people versus thin people, by noticing, for example, that overweight people are underrepresented in the media (in movies, magazines, ads, etc.) while thin people are represented as the norm.
(See also **body image**.)

Fellatio

Noun, from Latin *fellatio*, "fellatio," from *fellare*, "to suck"

Fellatio is better known as giving someone a blow job or giving head. It's a stimulation with the mouth and tongue of the penis and glans. Media and pornography place a lot of emphasis on oral sex, as if it were *the* most important sex practice. But this isn't true for everyone.

While some people like to receive or give fellatio, for others it's absolutely not a prerequisite for feeling pleasure. You should never feel pressured or coerced into giving or receiving an oral sex practice if you don't feel like it.

IN REALITY...

An antidepressant, a rejuvenating cream, a slimming ingredient... **semen**, if we're to believe some sources, could have miraculous virtues, prompting everyone to practice fellatio. But in reality, while it's expected that the person receiving fellatio can perceive certain advantages in it, much of this "information" on semen's miraculousness is false.

Femininity

Noun, from the adjective *feminine*, from Latin *femininus*, "concerning women"

Femininity refers to a set of physiological and psychological characteristics considered unique to women. Notice that the notion fits squarely into a feminine/masculine binary. In our society, the concept of **gender** tends to be divided into two groups: men and women, along with their respective **stereotypes**. For example, women are often associated with motherhood while men are linked with professional success.

When people think of femininity, they often imagine things like the color pink, gentleness, empathy, kindness or, inversely, hysteria. Masculinity is usually associated with the color blue, strength, anger and self-control. But if these so-called masculine traits are found in some women, do the latter become less feminine? And conversely, if so-called feminine traits appear in some males, are the latter less masculine? The answer is no, not at all.

Current changes in society (the rise of feminist and **LGBTQQIP2SAA+** movements, of feminist, gender and queer studies, etc.) are challenging these simplistic binary divisions and allowing us to take a different look at gender **identity** and standardized social roles. It's quite possible to have a man's body and identify as a woman. It's also possible to have the body of a woman and identify as a man. Femininity connects with **gender expression** when, for example, a person identifies with female attributes or as feminine.

THE BIRTH OF VENUS

Italian painter Sandro Botticelli's *The Birth of Venus*, circa 1485, has survived the ages as an allegory of femininity. It portrays a young woman emerging from the sea, naked, hiding her breasts and her sex with her hands and long hair. She stands on a seashell, staring, as if conscious of being observed. The woman is Venus, goddess of love and symbol of fertility, appearing "pure and virginal." One of the curators of a 2016 exhibition in London devoted entirely to Botticelli's idealization of women said of the *Venus* that she corresponds "to an image of perfect beauty conveyed since the Middle Ages...the Western woman, blond, of pale complexion, with a large forehead, clear eyes and a haughty bearing." Today the definition of feminity is much broader. It can be expressed in many different ways.

Fertility

Noun, from Middle French *fertilité*, "fact of being fertile"
from Latin *fertilitas*, "fruitfulness, fertility"

Fertility is the ability to reproduce. A child can be conceived if a person with a male sex produces viable sperm that fertilizes a mature egg from someone with female sex organs. Young people become able to procreate at **puberty**.

Not everyone is fertile, though—some people encounter fertility challenges.

For example, a person with a uterus who's affected by **endometriosis** has a higher risk of being infertile. Also, several **STDs** and **STIs**, including chlamydia and gonorrhea, can lead to infertility if they're not treated early enough.

In Canada, the birth rate has fallen dramatically in recent years. One of the reasons for this is that people with a uterus tend to have children much later in life, and fertility is at its peak between the ages of 20 and 24. In 1959, the average age for first childbirth was 23.2 years, while in 2019 it was 29.4 years. Another reason is that when the economy is slower, and the job market becomes precarious, people tend to postpone having children. Likely the global COVID-19 pandemic will have an effect on birth rates in countries around the world.

First Time(s)

First: ordinal numeral, from Old English *first*, "first, foremost"
Time: noun, from Old English *tīma*, "time, period"

First kisses, first desires, first fantasies, first masturbations, first caresses, first orgasms and so on. There will be more than one first time and probably more than one person to have a first time with. Your first intimate experience is important, but it won't necessarily determine your sexuality for the rest of your life. This way of seeing things is often hetero-centric (see **heterosexuality**), focusing on a heterosexual, cisgender couple composed of a man (with a penis) and a woman (with a vagina). A first time in this case means sexual activity involving a penis penetrating a vagina. But what happens when people don't identify with that model, or when someone's genitals are different from a penis or vagina?* Well, that doesn't change anything. First times are available for everyone, regardless of gender, genitals, sexual identity or sexual orientation. So don't worry too much about this first experience and simply view it as one of your (sexual) life stages.

There's no rule of thumb about exactly when you'll be ready to be intimate with someone else. Just be sure that when your first time does come, you feel good about entering a sexual relationship. It's a good idea to have it with someone who will respect you, your limits and your preferences, someone you think will have a "rhythm" that's similar to your own. It's also important to learn before-hand about **STDs** and **STIs** and the ways to protect yourself and to know about the contra-ceptive methods that will prevent an **unwanted pregnancy**.

* Different people may have different genitals. For example, an intersex person may have sexual attributes recognized as "female" (vagina, vulva, clitoris, ovaries, uterus) *and* "male" (penis, testicles). A person may have a penis formed through phalloplasty, a vagina through vaginoplasty or even a clitoris extension through metoidioplasty.

It's a good idea to have sex with someone who will respect you, your limits and your preferences, someone you think will have a "rhythm" that's similar to your own.

A perfect first time?

Unfortunately, a perfect first time doesn't exist! But there's nothing to prevent you from making a small list of expectations for your first time. You can fine-tune each time you have sex after that first time. You may discover a thousand other ways to live your sexuality in a fulfilling way!

Possible expectations might be to:

> have fun;
> try things out, explore your body and your partner's;
> trust yourself and learn your boundaries;
> relax, let go;
> say what you like and don't like;
> share your concerns with your partner if you feel the need to;
> be free to stop and start over, try something else or stop completely if you feel you've had enough or no longer want to continue;
> have the right to say no.

WHAT'S THE "NORMAL" AGE TO HAVE SEX FOR THE FIRST TIME?

Psychotherapist and sex therapist Mary Fisher doesn't use the word *virginity*. She says it's an outdated term in today's world, where it's accepted that intercourse is not the only way to have sex. "Instead of saying 'losing your virginity,' I use the words 'making your sexual debut.' Losing usually has a negative connotation, and your sexual debut should be a positive experience."

According to the US Department of Health and Human Services, 27 percent of high school students report being sexually active. People's first sexual experiences were classified as early if they happened between ages 13 and 15.5, and late if between 18 and 21 years old. But don't forget that these are averages and don't take into account the experiences of individuals.

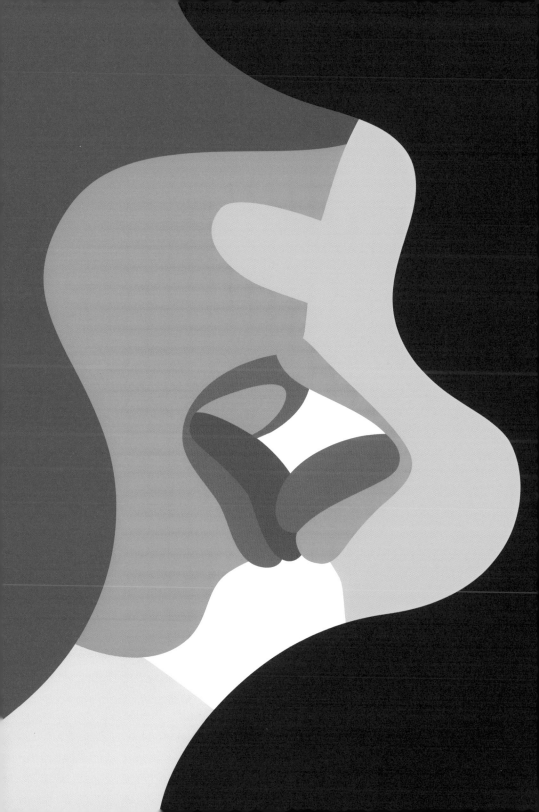

It can happen the first time (or anytime you have sex)

A body lives, breathes, makes noises, sweats, smells. During sex the intimacy with your partner(s) is very personal and has little in common with what we see in the movies. There may be awkward or uncomfortable moments, and you should feel like you can say something about them. Is your partner moving in a way that hurts you? Say it! Do you need a break to come to your senses, because a lot of new things just happened inside you? Say it! Would you like to be touched a certain way and your partner is doing it wrong? Say it! By speaking up when you need to, you respect yourself and, ultimately, make the moment even more enjoyable for everyone. It's important to watch and listen for signals like these from your partners. Everyone involved has the responsibility to be in tune with each other's wants, limits or discomfort.

There are numerous awkward things that can happen during a first time. The condom could get in the way of an erection. Vaginal flatulence or queefing could occur if the penetration is intense. If something like that happens, why not laugh about it together! And sex requires adjustments. Some positions are less comfortable than others, and if so, take the time to reposition yourselves. Penetration can hurt if there's not enough lubrication. Slow down. Go step by step. You have to try things to find out what you like.

LIKE SPAGHETTI

In a video for the science magazine *Curium*, actor and columnist Rosalie Bonenfant recounts her first time and compares it to...spaghetti! Frankly, that's a great analogy.
Let's recap:

> Your first spaghetti might not be the best, but there will be plenty of other opportunities for spaghetti later in your life (= It'll get better!).

> If you don't want spaghetti, no one should force you to have some (= No means no!).

> There's no specific age at which to eat your first spaghetti. Want to wait till you're 50 before having some? (= No problem!).

> What's important is that you actually feel like having spaghetti when you do get some (= Follow your desires!).

Foreplay

Fore: noun, from Old English *fore*, "before in time"
Play: verb, from Old English *plegan*, "engage in active exercise"

....

Sex is often mistakenly defined as a penis penetrating a vagina. That's because our societies are very heterocentric (focused on couples composed of a cisgender man and woman) and our cultures are flooded with heteronormative sexual representations (see **heterosexuality**). From a heterocentric perspective, the actions that precede sexual intercourse are called foreplay. They are gestures designed to slowly increase **arousal** until the moment of penetration. But kisses, caresses, massages, oral sex and masturbation are all sexual gestures that can put you "in the mood," and they can equate to a full sexual relationship whether accompanied by penetration or not. Two partners (or more!) can decide that having sexual intercourse together will consist only of oral sex, or kissing, or masturbating each other. And that's okay! In short, the word *foreplay* is misleading, as every sexual gesture you make constitutes a sexual experience in itself.

Free Instinctive Flow

Free: adjective, from Old English *frēo*, "free"
Instinct: noun, from Latin *instinctus*, "inspiration, impulse"
Flow: noun, from Old English *flōwan*, "to flow"

....

Free instinctive flow (FIF) is one of many ways to manage your period. This method, which originated in the United States, doesn't require a pad, tampon, menstrual cup or any hygienic protection. But how do you keep the blood from flowing then? You don't. When you feel that the menstrual blood is going to exit your body, you contract your perineum and retain it until you sit on the toilet. People who use FIF say when they have their period the body sends them a signal, like the need to urinate.

The reasons for using FIF are varied, but women who practice it say it allows them to have better control over their bodies, reconciles them with their periods, has a liberating aspect, means less contact with chemicals (since some menstrual pads and tampons contain chemicals; see **toxic shock syndrome**) and, of course, is environmentally friendly.

It should be noted that several doctors are skeptical about FIF. Martin Winckler, a former doctor and an author who specializes in women's health, says not all women succeed at mastering FIF and that you shouldn't feel guilty if you're one of them. His advice? "Test it and see." If it works and you feel comfortable using that method, that's the only thing that matters.

Friend with Benefits

Friend: noun, from Old English *frēond*, "friend, relative, loved one"
With: preposition, from Old English *wiþ*, "with, against"
Benefit: noun, from Anglo-Norman *benfet*, "well done," from
Old French *bienfaire*, "to do well," from *bien*, "well," and *faire*,
"to do"; modeled on Latin *bene facere*, "to do well"

The concept of a "friend with benefits" can be interpreted in several ways. Two people can have sex together and develop a friendship. Two people can be friends and develop a sexual relationship. Or two people can have an arrangement that mixes friendship and sex.

Friends with benefits are sometimes called fuck buddies, or fuck friends, but these are actually different concepts.

A friend with benefits is a person with whom you build a relationship, sharing time and activities (going to the movies or to a restaurant, sharing a dinner with mutual

Friends with benefits are sometimes called fuck buddies, or fuck friends, but these are actually different concepts.

friends), not just sex. In contrast, a fuck buddy is someone you know and have sex with on a regular basis but without any notion of friendship or of being a couple. It's a person with whom you'll share only sexual relations. The relationship won't usually leave the sexual framework. Most conversations between fuck friends will revolve around sexuality, not life in general, and they probably won't go on social outings together.

Friendship

Noun, from Old English *frēondscipe*, "friendship"

Although peer influence is already perceptible in preschool, during **adolescence** the circle of friends becomes very important. This is when we begin to better define ourselves, drawing inspiration from people who aren't our parents. At this age, points get across much better when they come from your friends rather than from your parents. Even if you love your **family** a lot, your network is growing during this time, and you seek freedom and different role models. The people around you play an essential role not just in shaping your personality but also in establishing social bonds that you might maintain throughout your life.

That being said, you have to know how and where to set your limits, even and especially with your friends. When you're among friends, you may feel the need to prove you can do things you wouldn't normally do. That's okay. It's exciting, and we all wish to impress and be recognized by our friends. And friends can have a big influence on you. Many people feel pressure to have sex as soon as possible because they think all their friends have. But people who brag about their sexual life and experiences are often exaggerating or fabricating events—because they too want to fit in!

In fact, it's normal during adolescence to act wilder than usual, because the limbic system (the part of the brain "concerned with instinct and mood" and that "controls the basic emotions (fear, pleasure, anger) and drives (hunger, sex, dominance, care of offspring)," according to the *New Oxford American Dictionary*) takes up all the space and prevents the brain from doing its job correctly. You stop thinking about the consequences of your actions. You wish to be cool, and you do everything to achieve that goal, even risky or silly things.

However—and this is important—friends, real ones, are people who are there during good times *and* bad times. They're people who never judge you for what you do and don't do or force you to act against your will.

GAY

GENDER

GENDER-AFFIRMING SURGERY

GENDER DYSPHORIA

GENDER EXPRESSION

GENDERFLUID

GENDER MARKETING

GENDER-NEUTRAL

GENDER NONCONFORMING

GENDER NORMATIVE

GENDERQUEER

GRAY (A)SEXUALITY

GYNECOLOGIST

G

Gay

Adjective and noun, from modern English *gay*,
"joyful," from Old French *gai*, "cheerful"

Although it sometimes means "cheerful or in a good mood," the adjective *gay* is usually used these days to describe a person who has a sexual or romantic attraction to a person of the same gender.

In premodern English, *gay* was used variously to refer to people who were nicely, colorfully dressed, then as a synonym of *noble* and *fair* (especially for women), then to characterize a light-headed, carefree attitude ("That gay, insulting man!") and finally as a pejorative synonym of *frivolous* and *hedonistic* (seeking pleasure at all costs). The more explicit term *homosexual* was only coined in the late 19th century and is attributed to the Hungarian journalist, writer and human-rights activist Károly Mária Kertbeny.

Gay in its modern sense took on a more political dimension in June 1969 when a violent police raid took place at the Stonewall Inn, a New York bar and gathering place for the **LGBTQQIP2SAA+** community (although, of course, the initialism LGBTQQIP2SAA+ didn't exist at the time). Several men were arrested. Over the next few days, New York witnessed what's now known as the Stonewall riots, spontaneous demonstrations in support of the LGBTQQIP2SAA+ crowd. A year later the first gay pride parade emerged from this event, with its marchers chanting slogans like "Gay pride, gay liberation!" a symbol of resistance to advocate people's rights to sexual and gender diversity.

In Canada, homosexuality was considered a crime punishable by law until 1969. The then prime minister, Pierre Trudeau, decriminalized sodomy (see **anal sex**) by ratifying the 1968–1969 Criminal Law Amendment Act (or Bill C-195). In presenting the bill to the media, Trudeau uttered a memorable justification: "There's no place for the state in the bedrooms of the nation." Nevertheless, it wasn't until 1987 that the notion of homosexuality was completely removed from the *Diagnostic and Statistical Manual of Mental Disorders (DSM)*, an influential (and controversial!) reference document used to diagnose mental disorders. In the United States, being openly gay was not illegal per se, but sodomy was illegal in many states, and many homosexuals were prohibited from entering the military. In 2011 then president Barack Obama repealed the Don't Ask, Don't Tell policy. In 2015 gay marriage was finally ruled legal by the US Supreme Court.

Gender

Noun, from Middle French *gendre*, "kind, type"

Gender defines the social differences that exist between men and women. Unlike sex, which is based on biological attributes (such as XX chromosomes in women and XY chromosomes in men), gender is based on roles, behaviors, and gender identities and expressions found in individuals.

For example, in our society people often associate the male gender with strength and the female gender with gentleness. But these are clichés, stereotypes! The definition of gender itself has evolved in the last few decades as society questions what really defines a man and a woman and tries to include all other gender identities and expressions.

In 1990 American theorist Judith Butler published *Gender Trouble*, a seminal book that stresses the fact that gender isn't innate but acquired. Professor and researcher Michel Dorais references Butler when he says,

Gender is like a pattern, reproduced over and over.

"We must understand gender like a socially learned and endlessly repeated performance." Gender therefore appears like a kind of pattern, reproduced over and over. It's possible to challenge the traditional gendered roles we've learned, as many advocates and allies try to do by systematically questioning gender norms and defending the concepts of fluid identities and sexualities. (See **psychological androgyny**.)

Still fully relevant today, theories of gender remain a work in progress.

Gender-Affirming Surgery

Gender: noun, from Old French *gendre*, "a kind, sort, category"
Affirming: adjective, from Latin *affirmare*, "to make steady, strengthen"
Surgery: noun, from Old French *surgerie*, "medical treatment of an operative nature"

Gender-affirming surgeries, formerly known as sex-realignment, sex-change or even bottom surgeries, are procedures that align or transition individuals to their true gender. Not all trans or nonbinary people choose to undergo gender-affirming surgeries, and these types of surgeries may have nothing to do with a person's sexual organs. Consider, for example, surgeries such as breast augmentation or facial masculinization. Gender-affirming surgeries are classified into two categories, upper-body (for example, masculinization of the torso via mastectomy) and lower-body (testicular prosthesis, phalloplasty, vaginoplasty, etc.).

Gender Dysphoria

Gender: Noun, from Middle French *gendre*, "kind, type"
Dysphoria: Noun, from Greek *dusphoria*, "pain that is hard to bear," from *dyshoros*, "hard to bear or carry"

The nonprofit organization GRIS-Montréal defines *gender dysphoria* as all the "negative emotions (anger, disgust, fear, sadness, etc.) a trans or nonbinary person may feel toward their gender **identity**." The term is often used in medicine and psychiatry, particularly in the *Diagnostic and Statistical Manual of Mental Disorders (DSM)*, frequently referred to as the "bible of psychiatry." Although gender dysphoria is typically associated with trans people, not all trans or nonbinary people experience it.

Gender Expression

Gender: noun, from Old French *gendre*, "a kind, sort, category"
Expression: noun, from Middle French *expression*, "action of expressing"

Regardless of their sex at birth, anyone has the right to explore their gender **identity**— female, male, both, neither or other—and express it through their clothes, their language and their way of thinking, being and acting in society. For example, someone can have a male sex but identify as more feminine and expresses that by wearing clothes usually reserved for the female sex, such as a skirt and high heels or makeup. This is called gender expression.

Genderfluid

Gender: noun, from Old French *gendre*, "a kind, sort, category"
Fluid: adjective, from Latin *fluidus*, "fluid, not fixed or rigid"

The adjective *fluid* is used in combination with the noun *gender* to describe the gender **identity** of people who fluctuate between several possibilities and find it difficult (or refuse) to define themselves with a specific gender identity. The terms *nonbinary gender* and *genderflux* are also used. Some people also see themselves as "fluid" in terms of their sexual orientation—it may change depending on the circumstances.

The term *fluid* in its noun form, in the context of this book, refers to a liquid secreted by the body and transmitted from one body to another during sexual relations. Examples of body fluids are saliva in kisses, semen in ejaculations, sweat when getting busy in bed (or elsewhere), vaginal lubrication when the vagina is aroused and stimulated, etc. In short, you can both *be* fluid and *have* fluids!

Gender Marketing

Gender: noun, from Old French *gendre*, "a kind, sort, category"
Marketing: from *to market*, from the noun *market* (from
Old Northern French *market*, "marketplace, trade")

Pink walls for little Lucy's bedroom and blue walls for little Oliver's. From baby's first pajamas to the electric razor, society assigns us a "natural" color based on our gender. Good luck to those who wish to extricate themselves from this designation! Yet according to Gavin Evans, author of *The Story of Color: An Exploration of the Hidden Messages of the Spectrum* (2017), parents were told during the late 19th and early 20th centuries to dress their boys in *pink* in order to "make men of them" and their daughters in *blue* to make them look more... feminine.

Historian Jo B. Paoletti, in *Pink and Blue: Telling the Boys from the Girls in America* (2012), writes that it was during the 1940s that it all turned around. After World War II, gender roles returned with a vengeance: men went back to work, women stayed at home, and a certain "normality" was reestablished. Brands then took the opportunity to breathe new life into a society recently traumatized by the horrors of war. They offered attractive, enjoyable products—perfumes, shampoos, creams, clothes. And why not have them in pink, to harmonize with the shiny new appliances?

TOYS FOR BOYS AND GIRLS

Pink dolls for girls and blue trucks for boys? "Enough!" says the campaign Let Toys Be Toys. From an early age, children are sensitive to stereotypes and risk conforming to them if they are not given the opportunity to explore other options.

This gendered marketing strategy quickly became lucrative. As a result, even today, when the time comes to buy a razor, soap or deodorant, women are presented with pink, turquoise, yellow or lilac packaging and designs, with round shapes reminiscent of feminine curves, accompanied by fruity, sweet scents and bearing names like Juicy Melon and Sweet Strawberries. On the men's side, we see mostly blue, metallic-silver and black products, with angular shapes and manly-sounding perfumes like Champ (never mind what an actual champ smells like...) or Lasting Legend!

CHIPS FOR WOMEN?

Gender marketing is targeting a specific group based on their gender (usually male or female) to sell them a product or service. In February 2018, Indra Nooyi, then CEO of PepsiCo, said in an interview for the *Freakonomics Radio* podcast that women don't eat chips the way men do. According to her, women are uncomfortable crunching their chips loudly and licking their fingers in public.

As a result, PepsiCo later announced the launch of a line of chips designed to be less messy, quieter and in a packaging format that could fit easily into a purse. It didn't take long for the news to notice, and Twitter went wild with #LadyDoritos, accusing PepsiCo of sexism. In response to her detractors, Nooyi claimed that the product was ultimately not going to be marketed and that it was only a "marketing test" to see how consumers would react to the concept. Many commentators have interpreted the move as an effective publicity stunt to get people to talk about the company.

Gender-Neutral

Gender: noun, from Old French *gendre*, "a kind, sort, category"
Neutral: adjective, from Latin *neutralis*, "of neuter gender"

Since June 2019, the Canadian government has allowed anyone who doesn't want to be identified as a man or a woman to choose a gender-neutral option and have an *X* rather than an *M* or an *F* entered on the Sex line of their passport. Many US states have begun offering nonbinary gender designations, but passports must indicate a male or female gender.

Being neutral means avoiding the use of words that automatically "classify" individuals, such as *sir* and *madam*, for example. Since March 21, 2018, the government agency Service Canada allows people to indicate how they want to be named.

> Being neutral means avoiding the use of words that automatically "classify" individuals.

Although many people disagree with this procedure, using people's preferred gender designation is a form of politeness and an easy adjustment to make. It helps people feel safer and more comfortable.

The use of a gender-neutral designation also shows a significant evolution in our society. The Canadian Centre for Gender and Sexual Diversity (CCGSD) "aspires to support and transform Canadian and Indigenous communities, from coast to coast, in a shared vision of a discrimination-free, gender and sexually diverse world."

Gender Nonconforming

Gender: noun, from Old French *gendre*, "a kind, sort, category"
Non: prefix, from Latin *non*, "not, by no means, not at all"
Conforming: adjective, from Old French *conformer*
"agree (to), make or be similar, be agreeable"

Western societies traditionally recognize two distinct genders, female and male, corresponding to two sexes, male (penis) and female (vagina). Many people expect others to conform to these standards, whether they apply to clothing (for example, dresses for women and pants for men), attitudes (virility for men and tenderness for women), professions and activities (women cooking and men working with wood) and so on. These expectations are also called **stereotypes**. People who are gender nonconforming don't wish or refuse to adhere to these stereotypes. They seek to redefine *gender* by embracing a number of traits without labeling them. By being playful and experimenting with different gender expectations, gender-nonconforming folk create new ways of interpreting these expectations. And gender nonconforming can also mean rejecting altogether the feminine/masculine dichotomy, inventing new genders or choosing not to identify with any gender at all.

Gender-Normative

Gender: noun, from Old French *gendre*, "a kind, sort, category"
Normative: adjective, from Latin *norma*, "rule"

A person is said to be gender normative when they adhere to or reinforce ideal standards of masculinity or femininity. For example, a trans woman (someone born with male genitals but who identifies as female) may want to be perceived as being feminine, while a trans man (someone born with female genitals but who identifies as male) may wish to associate himself with masculinity. Whether it's to reduce **gender dysphoria**, be recognized socially as a woman or man, or feel good about their appearance, identifying with a specific gender can be vital to some people.

Genderqueer

Gender: noun, from Old French *gendre*, "a kind, sort, category"
Queer: Adjective, possibly from German *quer*, "oblique, peculiar"

The term *genderqueer* describes someone whose chosen gender **identity** is neither masculine nor feminine but is between or beyond genders or some combination of genders.

Gray (A)sexuality

Gray or grey: adjective, from Old English *grǣg*, "gray-colored"
Asexuality: noun, from Greek privative prefix *a-*,
"without," and Latin *sexualis*, "sexual"

Gray asexuality or gray sexuality is used in reference to people (characterized as "gray-As" or "gray-aces") who locate themselves on the spectrum between **asexuality** and **sexuality**. Their sexual desire varies from low to more intense, depending on the time and circumstances in their lives. But then what difference is there between gray (a)sexuality and **demisexuality**?

Demisexuality involves a notion of attachment to the person you want to have sex with. Gray (a)sexuality doesn't involve a deep connection between people in order to have a successful sexual relationship.

Gynecologist

Noun, from Greek *gunaikos*, genitive form of *gunē*, "woman"
+ Greek -*logos*, "knowledge, word, reason"

Every person of female sex will, at one time or another, have to visit a gynecologist, who's a specialist in the functions and diseases of female reproductive organs. A visit to the gynecologist can be stressful when it's your first time—and even when you've been there before! This nervousness is normal.

Why should you consult a gynecologist? The first time it's usually because you intend to have sex in the near future or are already having sex and have questions. But ideally you would go there before having sex to learn about the different methods of **contraception** and perhaps be prescribed the one you wish to adopt. You would also discuss **STDs** or **STIs** with your gynecologist

so you understand the risks to which you're exposed if you don't use protection and in turn learn how to protect yourself effectively. You can also get this information from your family doctor or a public health nurse.

You will get referred to a gynecologist if you're experiencing problems with your periods (absence of periods, period pain, heavy bleeding, etc.). They will also make sure you get the proper sexual health exams, such as the Pap test, which is done to screen for cervical cancer (and can also be performed by a general practitioner or nurse). Women between the ages of 21 and 65 are encouraged to have the test done every two to three years.

HETEROSEXUALITY
HOMOPHOBIA
HOMOSEXUALITY

HORMONES
HYMEN
HYPERSEXUALIZATION

H

Heterosexuality

Noun, from the prefix of Greek origin *hetero-*, "other, different" + the noun *sexuality* (from Latin *sexualis*, "concerning sex," from *sexus*, "sex, gender")

Heterosexuality is the emotional, sexual or erotic attraction to people of the opposite sex.

Also consider the following connected words:

Heteronormativity is the assumption that everyone is heterosexual and that heterosexuality is the norm.

Heterosexism is discrimination against people with other sexual orientations, based on the assumption that everyone is heterosexual (*heterocentrism*). Behaviors, attitudes and representations (in ads, for example) emphasize heterosexuality and invalidate other sexual orientations.

Homophobia

Noun, from the prefix of Greek origin *homo-*, "same" + the combining form *-phobia* (from Greek *phobos*, "fear")

....

Homophobia is fear of or hatred toward people who identify as **LGBTQQIP2SAA+** or are presumed to be LGBTQQIP2SAA+. It can lead to violent words and actions. Many countries (about 70 in 2021) still consider homosexuality a crime. Worse yet, being homosexual is punishable by death in 12 countries! People may be homophobic for several reasons.

Religion
Many religious authorities have long regarded (and in many cases still regard) homosexuality as a disease and a sin.

History
Homosexuality has long been considered a disease in the medical community. And "conversion therapy" still exists today—a kind of "treatment" that aims to change homosexual people's sexual orientation and "get them back on track." These practices are banned by several Canadian provinces and 20 US states, as they are considered harmful to the health of their subjects.

Desire
Repressed homosexual desires can frighten people who feel them and cause them to react negatively, or even violently, toward homosexual people. This is called *internalized homophobia*.

Heterocentrism
Living in a society that assumes everyone should be heterosexual can breed homophobia.

Homosexuality

Noun, from the prefix of Greek origin *homo-*, "same" + the noun *sexuality* (from Latin *sexualis*, "concerning sex")

....

Homosexuality is the emotional, sexual or erotic attraction to people of the same sex. The words *homosexual* and *homosexuality* are often used today in a derogatory way, partly because the medical profession has long considered homosexuality a disease and an anomaly. The *Diagnostic and Statistical Manual of Mental Disorders (DSM)*, the reference manual used by North American psychiatrists, identified homosexuality as a mental disorder until 1987!

Some people discover their homosexuality when they're very young. For others, it happens later in life. You may never quite define or specify your **sexual orientation** (see also **genderfluid**) because you may not feel the need to. The important thing is to be comfortable with the the person or people you're attracted to, and to respect what you feel within yourself.

Hormones

Noun, from Greek *hormōn*, present participle of *horman*, "to set in motion"

....

Hormones are at the forefront of all transformations during puberty.

Adolescence is a time of great physical and psychological changes in your body. And hormones are at the forefront of all transformations. When the endocrine system initiates the secretion of sex hormones, everything kicks in following two main stages, adrenarche and gonadarche.

Adrenarche takes place shortly before puberty. It's when the adrenal glands come to maturity and sex glands become activated. Then puberty begins.

Gonadarche occurs when the sex glands come to maturity. It involves gonads, the ovaries and testes.

Hymen

Noun, from Latin *hymen*, "membrane"

....

This is a tiny piece of skin that gets a lot of attention! So much so that some women have surgery to reconstruct their lost hymen (called *hymenoplasty*).

The hymen is a thin fold of mucous membrane located at the entrance of the **vagina** and separating it from the **vulva** (although some women are born without it!). It's a kind of small barrier that in certain times and certain cultures was a symbol of purity and a token of **virginity**—and that's still the case today in some cultures.

Until the 1970s, in North America, young girls were expected to keep their hymen "intact" until their wedding night. The following morning the bedsheets were checked for the presence of a bloodstain that would prove the bride's loss of virginity. This "ceremony" was intended to certify to the groom that his descendants would indeed stem from him and not from another man with whom his wife may have had sexual relations before the marriage.

For these same reasons, internal "exams" were also performed on young girls to confirm the small membrane's presence. Hymens were (and still are in some places) serious business!

DIVINE VIRGINITY

In the book *Female Virginity: Myths, Fantasies, Emancipation*, French author Yvonne Knibiehler explains that, since ancient Greece, the virginity of female deities like Athena, Artemis and Hestia was linked to their ability to transmit divine messages. Knibiehler describes the Middle Ages as "the apex of [the idea of] female virginity" because female virginity then became a moral virtue (the will to remain a virgin demonstrated a strength of character, the will not to give in to the pleasures of the flesh), as well as a physical virtue (the celebration of a body remaining sexually "untouched").

TRUE OR FALSE?

1. **The hymen always breaks during your first sexual encounter.**
   FALSE: In fact, the hymen doesn't so much tear as it stretches to allow the penis (or a finger, a sex object such as a vibrator, etc.) to enter. A person with a vagina may well have stretched, damaged or even torn their hymen sometime in their childhood by playing sports, being active or simply by using tampons during their first periods. Even though the skin membrane is elastic, it is fragile!

2. **The hymen can bleed.**
   FALSE: The claim that all young girls bleed the first time they have sex is a myth. And if bleeding occurs, it probably isn't due to the tearing of the hymen but rather to the lack of lubrication in the vagina, which may suffer small cuts during penetration or by the rubbing of the penis, fingers or a sex object. Also be aware that some people are allergic to latex, and therefore if a latex condom is used during sex, it can cause skin reactions and small lesions.

3. **Penetration hurts.**
   FALSE: Penetration may hurt, but that is often due to stress or, again, lack of lubrication. If you feel pain, your partner may need to be more gentle. Take your time! During the first penetration, you're not sure what to expect, and you may be afraid and nervous. That is normal. It's a challenge to relax, let go and live in the moment with openness and curiosity.

   Ideally, talk with your partner(s) and express your fears. Laugh about them. That's right—*laugh* about them together! And try to make this experience a conscious and shared intimacy. (But note that it's different if you experience **vaginismus**.)

Hypersexualization

Noun, from the prefix of Greek origin *hyper-*, "over, excessive" and *sexual* (from Latin *sexualis*, "concerning sex")

Movies, videos and magazines are replete with images of sexualized bodies. Clothing ads frequently show half-naked models in languid and suggestive poses. "Sex sells," as they say. This is called hypersexualization, or *sexual objectification*. It is the trivialization (making something seem unimportant or superficial) of sexuality by applying its codes to topics that don't necessarily have to be sexualized.

Hypersexualization presupposes that people have to be sexy and sexually desirable to exist in society. And that's untrue!

Identity and Gender Identity

Identity: noun, from Latin *identitas*, "sameness," from *idem*, "the same"
Gender: noun, from Old French *gendre*, "a kind, sort, category"

Our identity is who we are. And that isn't determined overnight.

Your identity is who you are. And it isn't determined overnight. It's more like a work in progress that extends throughout your whole life. And identity building takes a giant leap when you go from childhood to adolescence. Identity includes everything that defines you as a person—your tastes, character, dreams and ambitions, ideas, flaws, strengths and weaknesses...in short, everything that makes you a human being!

As for *gender identity*, it's whether you identify with a masculine or feminine identity, with both, with neither or with yet another identity (**queer** or **nonbinary**, for example). A person can be female (have female sexual organs) and yet have a male gender identity. Another may be biologically male and not identify with any gender. (See **gender expression**.)

This can be a challenging time and you may have a lot of questions. Make sure you find the support you need.

Instagram

Proper noun, a blend of the adjective *instant* (from Latin *instans*, "standing by") and noun *telegram* (from combining forms of Greek origin *tele-*, "over a distance," and *-gram*, "written, recorded")

In 2020 this photo-and-video-sharing social media platform had more than one billion users. It offers an endless stream of photos of breathtaking landscapes, branded clothing you wish you could afford, mouthwatering ("and yet healthy!") recipes, yoga and fitness sessions performed in enchanting settings, and luminous, flawless selfies. Like a dream, right?

But Instagram has a darker side. Social media based on highly engaging visuals, such as Instagram and Snapchat, can create **anxiety** and feelings of insecurity among their users. Many young Instagrammers report feeling dissatisfied with their **body image**, a dissatisfaction that extends to their social life, achievements, popularity and so on. The social pressure already felt intensely during **adolescence** is increased tenfold by social media. It's hard—even as adults!—not to feel inadequate in front of so many perfect images, even though they don't reflect reality.

To stay safe on Instagram, here are a few things to keep in mind:

> Know the difference between a private and a public account. If you set your account as *private*, only the people you select will have access to your posts.

> Manage your interactions well. At all times, you can limit, filter and even block certain people or comments you consider inappropriate. Unfortunately, not all Instagram subscribers harbor good intentions.

> Manage your time wisely! Once you get started on Instagram, it's easy to lose track of time. And when that happens, you sacrifice other important areas of your life, like school, family, friends (in person!) and activities away from the screen. Give yourself a specific length of time you don't want to exceed—for example, one hour per day—to help you control your use of Instagram.

Intersex

Adjective and noun, from prefix of Latin origin *inter-*, "between, among," and noun *sex* (from Latin *sexus*, "sex, gender")

An intersex person has both female and male characteristics. The term *hermaphrodite* was historically used in scientific literature but is now considered pejorative, referring to "a medicalization of identity and gender expression."

According to the United Nations, there are more than 120 million intersex people in the world. They present the following types of differences:

1. Chromosomal

Chromosomes determine the **biological sex** of a person. All humans have 23 pairs of chromosomes. Males have XY chromosomes, and females have XX chromosomes. Y chromosomes determine the male sex, and X chromosomes the female sex. In intersex people, there are variations in the allocation of X's and Y's.

2. Hormonal

Intersex people may have differing levels of **hormones**. They can present more masculine physical characteristics while having a female sex or, conversely, more feminine characteristics while having a male sex. For example, an intersex woman might have a lot of facial hair and even a beard.

3. Reproductive

Differences may concern both genitality (a person's capacity to achieve orgasm) and the female and male **reproductive systems**. For example, it's possible for an intersex person to be born with a vagina *and* testicles. Or a penis *and* ovaries.

Intimacy

Noun, from *intimate*, from Latin *intimare*, "to relate, describe"

Intimacy is having a strong, deep bond with someone. It can take many forms. You can be intimate with friends when you exchange personal information and secrets. You can be intimate as a couple. Intimacy doesn't automatically connect with **sexuality** but, rather, comes from a great knowledge of the other person. You feel good with them, you confide your fears and insecurities, your joys and sorrows to them. And, of course, intimacy can be sexual in nature, which involves interacting with the other person emotionally (by feeling love, trust, respect, etc.) or physically. The more you progress in your romantic and sexual journey, the more you will understand what intimacy looks like for you and your partners.

KAMA SUTRA

LESBIAN
LGBTQQIP2SAA+
LGBTQQIP2SAA+ PARENTING
LOVE
LUBRICATION

K

Kama Sutra

Proper noun, from Sanskrit *kā́ma-sūtra*, "the ancient treatise *Kama Sutra*," from *kāma*, "love, desire," and *sūtra*, "treatise, aphorism; thread"

Attributed to the ancient Indian philosopher Vātsyāyana, the *Kama Sutra* (or *Kāmasūtra*) is considered by many to be the bible of love and sex. It was composed in India between 400 BCE and 300 CE and is made up of short texts on the topic of love and "the rules of marriage, the duties of the wife, the arts and worldly life, as well as the best way to seduce the wife of others."

According to Wendy Doniger, professor of the history of religions at the University of Chicago, this pioneering book was aimed at combating the religious discourse that confined sexuality "to the sole biological function of reproduction."

Although the *Kama Sutra*'s explicit illustrations occupy in reality only a modest portion of the book, it's definitely the most iconic part of the work today, giving it the aura of seduction, eroticism and exoticism that makes it one of the bestselling works in the history of printed text.

Austrian artist Bianca Tschaikner decided to revisit the all-time erotic bestseller that is the *Kama Sutra* with a colorful, kinky and queer version: the *MINISUTRA*! See biancatschaikner.com/minisutra.

Lesbian

Noun and adjective, from the Greek proper noun *Lesbos*,
the name of a Greek island in the Aegean Sea

A lesbian person identifies as a woman and feels a sexual
and romantic attraction to other women.

"Am I a lesbian?" If you ask the internet, you'll find a
fair number of forums, articles in women's media, quizzes
and even a 14-step guide, all offering help for answering
that question. But don't expect to find a definitive answer.
Sexual orientation is something personal and intimate. It
cannot be dictated by external standards or specifications.

Loving girls, or guys, or both, or nonbinary people, will only
ever be one part of your personality. What's more, sexual orientation can fluctuate over time.

What's important if you're asking yourself this question is
to pay attention to your feelings and be honest with yourself.
Dreams, private reflections and what you feel physically for
someone (excitement, desire) are usually trustworthy signals.

TRAILBLAZER

American photographer
Catherine Opie focuses
on the LGBTQQIP2SAA+
community in several
of her works. Her series
of portraits called
Being and Having
(1991) portrays her
lesbian friends.

According to Leila J. Rupp in
*Sapphistries: A Global History
of Love between Women*, it was
the sixth-century-BCE Greek
poet Sappho who really brought
attention to the pleasures between
women, through her poetry.
Athenian comedies used the words
lezbiazein and *lesbizein* to describe
sexual acts, in reference to the free
sexual culture of the Greek island
of Lesbos, where Sappho lived and
wrote. This eventually gave birth
to the modern word *lesbian*.

In 2008 residents of Lesbos
lodged a complaint with the
local court of law to denounce
the "usurpation" of the word by
gay women, "a qualifier [that]
reinforces female homosexual
tourism and harms heterosexual
tourism" in modern Lesbos. The
complainants even referred to the
poet Sappho, who they said was
evidently not gay because she
was "married to a man and had a
child." The complaint was deemed
inadmissible!

LGBTQQIP2SAA+

Initialism for lesbian, gay, bisexual, transgender, questioning, queer, intersex, pansexual, Two Spirit (2S), androgynous, asexual, with the symbol "+" meaning various potential inclusions in terms of gender and sexual diversity

The initialism LGBT has been used since the mid-1990s to refer to sexual minorities. It replaces the term *gay*, which typically applied to homosexual men and wasn't representative of sexual and gender **diversity**.

LGBT has since gained a few letters in order to be more inclusive.

The use of the initialism LGBTQQIP2SAA+ helps society recognize and acknowledge minority groups. But not everyone wants to be labeled with one or more of these "letters," and there are many nuances. Categorizations and labels are always tricky to use. While they definitely help non-LGBTQQIP2SAA+ people better understand the realities of LGBTQQIP2SAA+ people, they are unable to reflect the unique experiences of each and every person.

THE FAMILY IS GROWING

Several other terms have emerged in recent years. Here are a few that you might have seen:
> *Autosexual*: being sexually attracted to yourself
> *Skoliosexual*: being sexually attracted to nonbinary people
> *Sapiosexual*: being sexually attracted to a person's intelligence

LGBTQQIP2SAA+ Parenting

LGBTQQIP2SAA+: See opposite page for explanation.
Parenting: noun, from the noun *parent* (from Old French *parent*, "mother or father")

Families consisting of two mothers or two fathers are more and more common. *Same-sex parents* are two people of the same sex who start a family and raise one or more children together. So far, nothing really out of the ordinary here. Having children and starting a family is a desire common to many people, regardless of their sexual orientation.

Nevertheless, LGBTQQIP2SAA+ parenting is controversial worldwide. In 2012, in France, thousands of people gathered and demonstrated for months under the banner *Manif pour tous* (Protest for all). Their goal: to counter the French government's "marriage for all" bill, which sought to grant same-sex couples the right to marry and adopt children. This opposition gave rise to very heated debates. In Canada, same-sex marriage wasn't legalized until 2005.

A 2018 study by the US National Library of Medicine found that even though same-sex parents had higher levels of parenting stress, "their offspring did not differ in general health, emotional difficulties, coping behavior, or learning behavior when compared to the offspring of different-sex parents. However, lesbian mothers reported having concerns about raising children in a homophobic society, feeling pressured to 'justify the quality of their parenting than their heterosexual counterparts.'"

It's the prejudices toward LGBTQQIP2SAA+ parenting that are problematic, not these families.

FAMILIES THAT AREN'T SO DIFFERENT

A 2005 study by the American Psychological Association found no evidence that two same-sex parents are unable to raise children or that children of same-sex families are at a disadvantage compared to those of heterosexual parents. LGBTQQIP2SAA+ families are completely normal and experience the same challenges as any other family, the study concluded.

To learn more about LGBTQQIP2SAA+ families and find resources, visit familyequality.org.

Love

Noun and verb, from Old English *lufu*, "love"

Love is a powerful human feeling that can be divided into three categories: desire, attraction and attachment. These three forces trigger our **hormones** and make us experience emotions and physical reactions. Unless you're **aromantic**, love affects pretty much everyone, regardless of their age. It's a very intimate feeling and can be expressed in a very intense way. Love can be beautiful, sweet, uplifting.

But is it an obligation to be in love with the person you want to have sex with? Not at all. Although they may well intersect, **sexuality** and love are two different things. There's a difference between loving someone and desiring someone. Sometimes both dimensions may be present when you have a sexual relationship with someone. And that can be great, because the feeling of love has the capacity to generate strong emotions. And so the sexual dimension of your relationship may become more and more important. But it doesn't have to be.

> Just because you feel you love a person so much your heart could explode doesn't mean you have to do everything they want.

However, just because you feel you love a person so much your heart could explode doesn't mean you have to do everything they want. This is true in all areas of life, and it's especially true in matters of sexuality. A person who truly loves you will always respect when you say "no" and never ask you to do something you don't want to do because "that's what love is." Uh-uh. Love can be expressed in myriad ways, and the first way is by respecting the other.

Lubrication

Noun, from the verb *to lubricate* (from Latin *lubricare*, "to make slippery")

··

When a person with female sexual organs is sexually aroused, the walls of their vagina "sweat" because of the activation of the Skene's glands. A second transparent liquid flows from the Bartholin's glands located on both sides of the vulva. These substances make it easier for the penis to penetrate the vagina during sex and also make it easier for fingers or a sex toy to penetrate.

Vaginal lubrication associated with sexual arousal is colloquially known as *love juice*. But some people don't have that natural reponse to arousal. This isn't necessarily a problem. If you find that happening, just be sure that arousal and sexual stimulation are sufficient before sex. If they are and your lubrication is still lacking, lubricants (sold in all drugstores) can be used.

Lubrication (or the lack of it) isn't directly related to sexual pleasure.

Note that lubrication (or the lack of it) isn't automatically tied to sexual pleasure, in terms of quality *or* quantity. Indeed, some people may not experience sexual arousal but nonetheless notice some physical arousal, such as lubrication in the vagina.

SQUIRTERS: YES BUT NO

A certain image, frequently highlighted in **pornography**, activates the sexual imagination of many people: the infamous "squirters." Squirters are people with a vagina who are shown having an orgasm and ejaculating with great force. Indeed, people of the female sex also ejaculate (see **ejaculation**), but since it's usually pretty discreet, their sexual partners might not always notice. Squirters ejaculate in a more spectacular way. It's uncommon but remains a sexual fantasy for many people, especially for men. That said, female ejaculation, in both quality and quantity, has little to do with your desire and arousal.

MASCULINITY
MASTURBATION
MENSTRUAL CUP
MENSTRUAL CYCLE
MENSTRUAL PAD

MENSTRUAL UNDERWEAR (PERIOD PANTIES)
MENSTRUATION
#METOO
MISGENDER
MUSCLE TALK

Masculinity

Noun, from the adjective *masculine*, from Old French *masculine*, "male"

Masculinity could be defined as the ultimate representation of what a man should be. The word *should* is important here, because in reality, just because you're a man or have a masculine gender doesn't mean you feel "masculine" or "manly."

Masculinity as we know it is often portrayed with the image of a strong, virile, courageous **cisgender** man who isn't afraid of anything and is always in control of his emotions. This is called a **stereotype**—an idealized, unrealistic representation.

Just because you're a man or have a male gender doesn't mean that you feel "masculine."

So if you don't match that image, does it mean you're less—or not—masculine? No. There are masculine women, just as there are feminine men. There are people who identify as nonbinary but who describe themselves as being more masculine or more feminine. In short, masculinity is an elastic qualifier that fits people differently (if at all). And it's been proven that breaking away from binary stereotypes (man/woman, masculinity/femininity) is beneficial for a person and allows them to be more fluid in their way of being and behaving (see **psychological androgyny**).

THE INFAMOUS "TOXIC MASCULINITY"!

Toxic masculinity is a narrow and oppressive description of manhood. Society sets certain standards that males "must" follow if they are to be "real men." But in reality these standards are well-anchored stereotypes, and they become toxic because they may make those who feel uncomfortable with those standards feel marginalized or abnormal.

Masturbation

Noun, from Latin *masturbatio*, "self-pleasuring"

From ancient Greece until today, many religions have condemned masturbation. At the beginning of the 18th century, a book called *Onania*, attributed by some to Balthasar Bekker and by others to John Marten, was published in London. It identified masturbation, or "onanism" (from a character named Onan in the Old Testament), as the root of all evils—deafness, blindness, sterility, dementia and so on. The full title of the book? *Onania: or, The Heinous Sin of Self-Pollution, and All Its Frightful Consequences, in Both Sexes, Consider'd, With Spiritual and Physical Advice to Those Who Have Already Injur'd Themselves by This Abominable Practice.* Scary, isn't it?

The following century, remedies, potions, ointments, medication and even mechanical devices were developed to prevent people from masturbating. A real museum of horrors existed: rings with sharp metal tips placed on the penis so it would be pricked should an erection occur and devices that delivered electric shocks should the penis be affected by a sudden and involuntary erection (during sleep, for example).

Even today masturbation is a taboo subject. Many people still giggle, blush or roll their eyes at the mention of it. Nevertheless, the vast majority of people will masturbate at one time or another. Starting in our mother's womb, we begin exploring our bodies and the pleasures we can experience when touching ourselves. Between the ages of two and five, children often touch, rub and stroke their genitals—although the motivation at that time isn't exactly the same as it is in adolescence and adulthood. But the idea remains the same—to make ourselves feel good.

IN MAY, DO WHAT YOU MAY

Since 1995 in the United States, the month of May has been the time to talk openly masturbation. National Masturbation Day was launched on May 7 in support of former US surgeon general Joycelyn Elders, who lost her job during Bill Clinton's presidency after proposing that school curricula incorporate the subject of masturbation. The celebration was extended to encompass the whole month of May, encouraging conversations about masturbation to get rid of taboos about it and help more and more people understand that masturbation is a completely normal sexual activity to be practiced without fear.

Masturbation is useful: it relaxes, lowers stress, improves sleep, calms menstrual pains. All of this, just by masturbating!

Masturbating also allows you to get to know your body better, to appreciate it and understand what makes it feel good. It also allows you to explore your erotic and romantic imagination. It informs you about your preferences and can even answer questions you might have about your **sexual orientation**. Are you thinking of a boy in your class when masturbating? Or a girl? Or both? You're not thinking of anyone? It's all good.

Masturbating has a big impact on your sexuality, because if you know how your body reacts and what makes it happy, the chances of experiencing **pleasure** with your partner(s) increase. Masturbating also allows you to vary your sexual practices and explore your sexuality. There is more than one way to experience your sexuality in life...and it's not all about intercourse or sexual interactions with other people.

Masturbation is a great opportunity to explore sexuality on your own, but it can also be practiced in pairs, exploring and giving pleasure to each other's bodies.

Nevertheless, while masturbation offers many advantages, it's not mandatory. Don't want to masturbate? This is perfectly fine—no one is forcing you to.

Menstrual Cup

Menstrual: adjective, from Latin *menstrualis*,
"monthly; concerning menstruation"
Cup: noun, from Old English *cuppe*, "small drinking vessel"

Nope, a menstrual cup isn't a trophy, like the Stanley Cup or the FIFA World Cup, awarded to someone who has managed their period perfectly! It's an eco-friendly and affordable tool to replace good old tampons.

A menstrual cup is a small, flexible silicone container with a narrow rod at the end so you can easily remove it. You fold the cup in half or into the shape of a U and insert it into your vagina. Once it's inside, you turn it around to seat it properly, then release it so it opens up and regains its original shape. Once it's in place, you can go about your business. Just remember to remove it after a few hours (between 8 to 12 hours maximum). Empty it, then either replace it or rinse it and put it back in. If the cup is reusable (some models are disposable), you must clean it between each menstrual cycle. It must be sterilized too—immerse it in boiling water and clean it with a pH-neutral soap (see **vaginal flora**).

If you care about your environmental impact, menstrual cups may be a great choice. When properly taken care of, they can last for several years, unlike disposable tampons and pads, which create a considerable amount of waste. A few stats? Each year, according to the US National Women's Health Network, 12 billion menstrual pads and seven million tampons are thrown away in the United States alone. In addition, tampons and pads cost a lot of money. In 2019 the global feminine-hygiene products market was worth $26 billion.

Every year 12 billion menstrual pads and seven million tampons are thrown away in the United States alone.

Using and handling menstrual cups requires some getting used to. But the method is popular and gives many users the feeling that they can forget about their period. Others find it uncomfortable. You have to know your body well and not be grossed out by menstrual blood, since some of it can get on your fingers when you empty the cup. But if you want to adopt a relatively natural method that allows you to be in tune with your periods, get to know your body more and tame your aversion to menstrual blood (it's just a little bit of blood!), menstrual cups are the way to go. Remember to practice good hygiene and empty the cup regularly.

PERIOD ART

In 2017, BuzzFeed's *Ladylike* team collaborated with artist Sarah Levy. The result? Menstrual blood was used as art material! Yep. And to obtain it, they used menstrual cups. Levy is also known for her portrait of Donald Trump, also made with her menstrual blood.

LISTEN

The *Heavy Flow* podcast hosted by Amanda Laird answers every question you may have about your period, including how to pick the best menstrual cup. Visit amandalaird.ca/the-heavy-flow-podcast.

Menstrual Cycle

Menstrual: adjective, from Latin *menstrualis*, "monthly; concerning menstruation"
Cycle: noun, from Latin *cyclus*, "circle; cycle"

A menstrual cycle typically lasts from 21 to 35 days. The average is 28 days, but duration may vary from month to month. Fluctuations are more common during adolescence and premenopause. A cycle has three phases:

1. Periods and preovulation (or follicular phase)
2. Ovulation (or ovulatory phase)
3. Luteal (or premenstrual) phase

Periods and preovulation
(or follicular phase)

Your period's first day determines the remainder of the menstrual cycle. If you don't have sexual intercourse or use contraception or if there is no contact between the sperm and the egg, there's no fertilization. The protective layer that formed on the inner walls of the uterus in order to receive a possible pregnancy then self-destructs and flows out as blood and tissue. The blood flow can last from three to eight days. For a majority of people, it lasts five days. During the first few days, the flow is more abundant, and then it eases off until it stops. This phase is called the follicular phase because the body produces follicles (small receptacles) that release eggs for the purpose of getting them fertilized. In most girls and women, the phase lasts about 16 days.

Ovulation (or ovulatory phase)

This phase begins about halfway through the cycle, either around the 14th or 15th day. The brain sends a signal that causes **hormone** levels to increase, and the egg, which has become mature and is therefore ready to be fertilized, is released to settle in the **fallopian tube**. This is where it can come into contact with the sperm, if the person has had sex without contraception. The egg stays there for about 24 hours, dissolving if there's no fertilization.

Luteal (or premenstrual) phase

This phase is from ovulation until the end of the cycle — from the 14th or 15th day of the cycle to the 28th day. The brain then initiates a hormonal process that revives endometrial production in anticipation of another possible pregnancy. It's a process that repeats itself every month, which is why it's called a cycle. For more information, visit YourPeriod.ca.

Menstrual Pad

Menstrual: adjective, from Latin *menstrualis*, "monthly; concerning menstruation"
Pad: noun, possibly from Low German *pad*, "soul of the foot"

Pads are probably the most common way to manage your period. They come in a variety of sizes and brands: regular, thin, ultra-thin, with or without "wings," maxi or super for overnight use or mini for the end of your cycle. They can be found almost everywhere, at the grocery store, the pharmacy and the convenience store.

How do they work? Very simple. They stick to the inside of your underwear, sometimes with "wings" that fold down on the sides to help prevent blood from staining the fabric (since when you move, the pads move too. Pads are a bit like mini diapers, only thinner, and they absorb the menstrual flow.

> Regular, thin, ultra-thin, with or without "wings," maxi or super for overnight use or mini for the end of your cycle.

Some people find that pads aren't the most comfortable way to manage their periods, but many get used to them and find them convenient. And yes, the smell can be a bit unpleasant. It's caused by the blood coming in contact with air and oxidizing. Pads can be changed as often as you need to feel comfortable, but make sure not to keep them on for more than four to six hours.

Menstrual pads use a lot of plastic! That's why there are also washable versions.

WASHABLE PADS

The very first pads used by women were washable. Current versions may be better designed and more practical, but they're used in much the same way as in the past. Washable (reusable) menstrual pads are made from natural products like hemp and cotton and, unlike disposable pads from many brands, are bleach-free.

Be aware that in Canada and the United States, companies that make pads don't have to list the materials in them, despite some of them having the potential to cause reactions and infections. This is why many people turn toward more natural methods, such as pads made out of cloth.

Several companies offer "starter kits" with everything you need to take care of your period, including an airtight bag in which to place used pads. True, washable pads can be a bit expensive, but in the long run they are cheaper than disposable ones. And what's more, they are good for the environment.

Menstrual Underwear
(Period Panties)

Menstrual: adjective, from Latin *menstrualis*,
"monthly; concerning menstruation"
Underwear: noun, from prefix *under-* + *wear* (from Old English *werian*, "to dress")
Period: noun, from Middle French *periode*, "time interval"
Panties: plural noun, from *pant(aloons)* (from French *pantalons*, "pants")

A number of companies offer period-proof underwear called menstrual underwear or period panties. These are panties with a thick bottom layer designed to absorb menstrual flow. They're comfortable and nice-looking but can be expensive (between $30 and $50 USD). They're a long-term investment, as these panties are washable and reusable panties, so can last for years.

For some people, however, the protection afforded by the underwear may not be enough to absorb all menstrual discharge. If that's the case for you, try adding a second layer of protection (a washable or disposable menstrual pad) to your underwear.

Menstruation

Noun, from Latin *menstrua* (plural of *menstruum*),
"menstrual discharge," from *menstruus*, "monthly"

More than half of the people in the world menstruate—or, as it's more commonly described, get their period. That's a lot of people! Yet today millions of menstruating people still don't have access to hygienic protection. In Canada menstrual hygiene products were taxed until 2015 because they were considered "luxury items"!

In a 2018 survey of 1,500 women in the United States, 55 percent admitted to feeling embarrassed and shameful when having their periods, and 42 percent had experienced situations in which people ridiculed them for having their periods. But menstruation is natural and normal.

What is the point of menstruation?

Starting at puberty and ending with meno-pause, there is a monthly cycle in which a woman's body prepares for possible preg-nancy and then sheds tissue when pregnancy doesn't occur. Periods are a part of women's fertility cycles. Martin Winckler, a former doctor and a women's health specialist, likens this process to a molt.

Snakes, for example, grow an inner skin that will replace their external skin when the time comes for them to molt. Likewise, in women the endometrium (the mucous membrane that covers the lining of the uterus) thickens at the start of the menstrual cycle to accommodate an eventual embryo. At the end of the cycle, if no embryo has implanted, a large part of that mucous membrane peels off and becomes the period.

Many people wonder if they can have sex during their period. The answer is absolutely! All the more so, since having an orgasm is proven to relieve menstrual pain. Furthermore, menstrual blood—which contains vaginal secretions—makes it easier for a finger, penis or sex toy to penetrate the vagina. So there's no downside to having sex during your period. If you feel comfortable, your menstrual pain is not too intense and you're sexually aroused, allow yourself a little fun!

The typical amount of blood that flows during a period is two to three tablespoons. It may seem like more than that because menstrual blood is accompanied by secretions. But some women do experience abnormally heavy flow, which is called menorrhagia.

FUNNY NOT-SO-FUNNY STORIES...

For a long time people thought that red-haired women were permanently menstruating—hence the color of their hair!

Another strange misconception was that a menstruating person who prepared mayonnaise would automatically spoil it.

A Slavic tradition was for mothers to slap their daughters during their first period so they would have regular periods from then on and their flushed cheeks would conceal their monthly "indisposition."

#MeToo

(pronounced "hashtag"): noun, from *hash (sign)*, "the symbol #"
Me: personal pronoun, from Old English *mē*
Too: adverb, from Old English *tō*

On October 15, 2017, actor Alyssa Milano promoted the Me Too movement on Twitter, encouraging all people who had been victims of sexual assault or sexual harassment to post about their experience and raise awareness. Within hours, millions of #MeToo tweets had been posted.

It wasn't Milano who originated the Me Too movement, but Tarana Burke, founder and director of Just BE Inc., a New York organization focused on the health, well-being and safety of young women of color. Burke launched the movement in 2007, to raise awareness of victims of sexual assault. Ten years later, the movement had become so powerful and generated so many repercussions internationally that people often refer now to pre- and post-#MeToo eras.

Misgender

Verb, from the prefix of Germanic origin *mis-*, "wrongly," and the noun *gender* (from Old French *gendre*, "a kind, sort, category")

To misgender is to label a person, often trans or **nonbinary**, the wrong way—for example, using the wrong gender (often male or female but possibly also **agender**) or the wrong **pronoun** (*he/him, she/her* or *they/them*), or continuing to use the name a trans person had before transitioning (a mistake called **deadnaming**).

While most people misgender people because of clumsiness, ignorance or embarrassment, others do it on purpose to make the person feel inadequate. Remember, it's easy to ask and remember how a person wishes to be identified (their preferred pronoun). Easy as one, two, three!

A FEW EXAMPLES

Thomas, whose legal first name was Julie before his transition, is still referred to as Julie by his mother, who refuses to accept his gender transition.

At work, Eric informs her colleagues that from now on she wants to call herself Anne and asks that they use the pronoun *she* to refer to her, in line with what Anne recognizes as her true female identity. Her colleague Matthew, however, continues to use the pronoun *he* because he's uncomfortable with the change.

Violet considers themself neither a woman nor a man. The label *nonbinary*, as well as the pronouns *they*, *them* and *themself*, suits them. But although Violet has been clear with others about their preferences, the people around them have difficulty accepting it and often continue to use the pronouns *she*, *her* and *herself* to speak of Violet.

Muscle Talk

Muscle: noun, from Middle French *muscle*, "muscle"
Talk: noun, from Old English *tealcian*, "to talk"

....

Comparable to young girls' **fat talk**, muscle talk is the tendency of (mostly) males to wish for the excessive development of their musculature, often to the point of obsession. The media and advertisers are no strangers to this phenomenon.

According to a 2012 study of 3,000 people, the number of images of naked, muscular men in ads has increased significantly since the 1980s. The same study revealed that children's action figures have evolved to become extremely muscular, idealized bodies that look more like bodybuilders than average people. Because of that, young people, especially boys, may develop body dissatisfaction (not loving your body) or **body dysmorphia** (a mental disorder characterized by focusing on how the body or a part of the body is inadequate or has defects).

NETFLIX AND CHILL
NONBINARY
NONMONOGAMY
NORMAL
NUDITY

ODOR
ONE-NIGHT STAND
ORAL SEX
ORGASM
OVARY

Netflix and Chill

This expression allegedly emerged around 2009 on Twitter through an account named NoFaceNina, linked to a subscriber named La Shanda Rene Foster. Its original meaning apparently wasn't sexual and simply meant, quite literally, settling down to watch a movie on the popular streaming platform and relaxing! The meaning shifted in 2015 and took on a sexual connotation. Today, if someone sends you an invitation to "Netflix and chill," they're asking you to watch a movie or show on Netflix *and*, hopefully, end the evening with sex.

Nonbinary

Adjective, from the prefix of Latin origin *non-*, "not," and the adjective *binary* (from Latin *binarius*, "of two")

People who identify as *nonbinary* have a **gender** that doesn't fall under the category of male or female. It's an umbrella term for for a number of identities outside of male and female. It can include people who identify as **genderqueer**, **genderfluid** or **agender**.

Nonmonogamy

Noun, from the prefix of Latin origin *non-*, "not," and *monogamy* (from French *monogamie*, "state of being married to one person")

Monogamy is the state of being in a relationship with just one person, with sexual and romantic fidelity. Infidelity is usually not acceptable in monogamous relationships and is often considered a form of betrayal.

Nonmonogamy, by contrast, means having more than one partner or being in a relationship but having sexual or romantic relationships with other people too. It doesn't necessarily cancel fidelity—a person can decide to have several partners while remaining in a relationship with the same person.

However, the definition of fidelity, or faithfulness, is not absolute. Am I still faithful if I kiss someone other than my partner? What if I have sex with someone else? Where is the line between fidelity and infidelity? It's up to the people inside the romantic or sexual relationship to determine it together.

Normal

Adjective, from Latin *normalis*, "following a rule"

．．．

When you're a teenager, you often feel abnormal. And that's...normal!

It's hard to know where we stand in relation to our friends, the people we hang out with and our parents, as we don't always openly discuss issues of **sexuality** or **body image**. Normality is a very, very relative notion. And remember that society actively "normalizes" bodies, behaviors, tastes and attitudes. Every day we are shown models that don't correspond to us.

So what to do with all of this?

You have to try to keep a critical mind about what's presented to you in the media, and learn to deal with your body image. It isn't easy, especially when you're bombarded every day with images of supposedly perfect bodies that you often can't identify with. Normality is not what is presented in the media. What *is* normal, and what you have to deal with, is your own body, both the good and the bad, its flaws and its strengths. Your body has little to do with the prefabricated images that corporations try to sell to you, often without your noticing it.

As to the "normality" of lived experiences, such as your first kiss, your first sexual relationship, your sexual preferences or orientation, it can be different for each person (see **first time(s)**). It's not about what society thinks is normal but what feels healthy for you and your partners. Be sure you move at your own pace. Sometimes you might think people around you have already lived it all. But that's often not the case. The same questions swirl in the heads of a lot of people!

"Is it normal if I haven't kissed someone yet?"
"Is it normal if I haven't had sex yet?"
"Are my periods normal?"
"Is my penis normal?"
"Are my breasts normal?"
"Is it normal not to know if I am attracted to girls or to boys?"
"Is it normal to feel like a girl when I was born into a boy's body, or like a boy when I was born into a girl's body?"

Nudity

Noun, from French *nudité*, "nakedness"

....

Nudity, or nakedness, refers to being unclothed or uncovered. For some people, nudity is a source of *empowerment* (taking control of your own life), but for others, nudity is synonymous with vulnerability.

It's not always easy to accept your body in the face of difficult-to-achieve beauty standards, even if each body is uniquely beautiful (see **beauty**). It's even less easy to get naked in front of your sexual partner(s) when you're about to have sex for the first time. We all hope that others will accept and appreciate us, regardless of the body we have—and that's how it should be!

Nudity can also be private or public. On the one hand, taking nude selfies is fine, but what if someone else gets access to these images? And what if those photos are made public without your consent?

On the other hand, some people share photos or videos of themselves partially or completely naked because their bodies are a source of pride to them and they're comfortable with what they're doing.

On the *Refinery29* website, see "How To Send Nudes (Mostly) Safely," which describes how to take erotic photos safely.

Odor

Noun, from Anglo-Norman French *odour*, "scent"

....

A body emits odors, from perspiration, breath, saliva, the skin and sexual organs. These smells play a role in how attracted (or not) you feel to a person (see **physical and sexual attraction**). While some odors exhilarate us, others are downright repugnant. Our reactions to smells, our senses, inform us of what we like and dislike.

During sex your body moves, increases in temperature and secretes fluids that have special scents. Sanitized sex, where everything is clean and smooth like in the movies, only exists...in the movies! In real life, sex is

> Sanitized sex, where everything is clean and smooth like in the movies, only exists... in the movies!

full of with noises, smells, physical reactions that can be surprising (panting very hard, screaming, etc.), and none of it has to be repressed. It's all part of the game!

One-Night Stand

One: cardinal numeral, from Old English *ān*, "one"
Night: noun, from Old English *niht*, "night"
Stand: noun, from Old English *standan*, "to stand, take place"

....

Having a one-night stand means having a one-time sexual encounter, for an evening or a day, often with a stranger or someone you just met.

The original meaning, from the late 19th century, was "a single performance of a play or show, especially by a touring company." Its sexual meaning probably emerged in the late 1950s.

(See also **friend with benefits**.)

Oral Sex

Oral: adjective, from Latin *oralis*, "of the mouth," from *os*, "mouth"
Sex: noun, from Latin *sexus*, "sex, gender"

Sex is usually associated with penetration, but **sexuality** is so much more than that. There are many ways you can have fun and feel **pleasure**. Oral sex is a good example. It involves using your mouth and tongue on your partner's penis, clitoris or anus to give them pleasure. Whether it's **fellatio, cunnilingus** or anilingus (see **anal sex**), there are plenty of ways for you to have fun!

Oral sex is an intimate act that can be awkward at first. But if you let yourself go, feel the desire for it and trust your partner, it can be extremely pleasant. You can view oral sex as a different way to explore sexuality and please your partner, but also as a way to better understand your partner's sexuality and sexual preferences. And vice versa! But one thing is very important to remember: fellatio, cunnilingus or anilingus should never be an obligation or reward. They are are simply other ways to experience pleasure and to explore the other's body with their **consent**. Engage in oral sex only if you want to.

You should also know that just because there's no penetration doesn't mean there's no risk of catching or transmitting **STDs** or **STIs**. Take genital or labial herpes, for example. You can get other STDs or STIs through oral sex: chlamydia, gonorrhea, syphilis and HPV. It's always better to protect yourself, and the **dental dam** is a good way to do this. Condoms can also be used for oral sex.

"THE INFALLIBLE WAY TO TAKE HIM TO CLOUD NINE!"

You've probably seen magazine articles with titles like this, promising tips for performing out-of-this-world fellatio. But this is problematic for several reasons.

First, it implies that every woman (or man) should offer fellatio, and that anybody with a penis dreams of receiving one.

Second, it steals the spotlight from cunnilingus, a practice much less talked about. In contrast, fellatio is often portrayed as "the cement holding the couple together."

Finally, it completely sets aside anilingus, an even lesser-known practice (although a lot of people practice it!) that can provide as much pleasure as cunnilingus and fellatio.

Long story short, the best sex techniques are the ones that turn you and your sexual partner(s) on and make all of you feel good.

Orgasm

Noun, from Latin *orgasmus*, "orgasm, spasm," from
Greek *orgasmos*, "excitement, swelling"

An orgasm is the body's physiological response when **arousal** is at its peak. In a way, it's one of the ultimate goals of sex—to **climax**. Having an orgasm is typically pleasing, fun, delightful...

But remember, you don't necessarily have an orgasm during sex. Sometimes you really would like it to happen, you feel the desire and the excitement happening, and it seems like it's just around the corner and...nope, it doesn't happen. Don't worry. It's possible you were just tired, stressed, not focused enough. The rhythm of the penetration, for example, might not have been fast or slow enough, the caresses and stimulation of certain areas not fine-tuned, and so on.

Several things can prevent you from reaching orgasm. And unless you can never attain one and develop a specific problem (called anorgasmia, the pathological inability to achieve orgasm), don't worry about it. It may simply be a matter of adjusting the timing or relaxation level and making other tiny changes. Reaching orgasm can only be achieved by knowing your body (including during solo masturbation!) and your sexual partner's body.

(See also **masturbation**.)

> You don't always have an orgasm during sex.

Ovary

Noun, from Latin *ovarium*, "ovary," from *ovum*, "egg"

The ovaries are two small glands located at the end of the **fallopian tubes** and attached to the **uterus**. Inside the ovaries are the oocytes, the sex cells of women, which turn into eggs when ovulating. Ovaries also generate important hormones: estrogen and progesterone, which cause the **menstrual cycle** (see **hormones**).

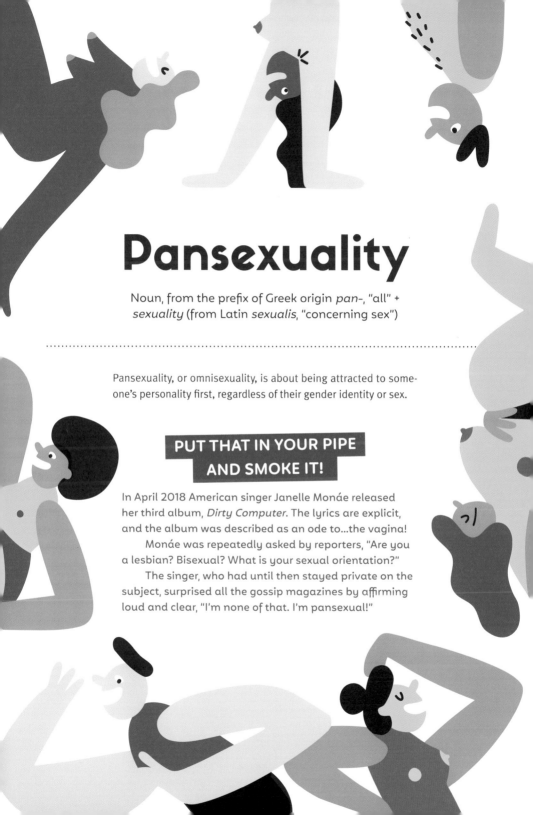

Pansexuality

Noun, from the prefix of Greek origin *pan-*, "all" + *sexuality* (from Latin *sexualis*, "concerning sex")

Pansexuality, or omnisexuality, is about being attracted to someone's personality first, regardless of their gender identity or sex.

PUT THAT IN YOUR PIPE AND SMOKE IT!

In April 2018 American singer Janelle Monáe released her third album, *Dirty Computer*. The lyrics are explicit, and the album was described as an ode to...the vagina!

Monáe was repeatedly asked by reporters, "Are you a lesbian? Bisexual? What is your sexual orientation?"

The singer, who had until then stayed private on the subject, surprised all the gossip magazines by affirming loud and clear, "I'm none of that. I'm pansexual!"

Penis

Noun, from Latin *penis*, "tail or penis"

....

Whether big or small, long or short, wide or narrow, curved or straight, veiny or smooth, pink, brown or purple, circumcised* or not, the male sex is the victim of different stereotypes: it has to be big, hard, efficient, ready for anything, available on demand, endowed with unending erections and never tired!

Let's start by saying that the size of the penis isn't necessarily linked to sexual pleasure. To say otherwise would be to say that sex is all about penetration, which it isn't. Obviously, penetration by a large penis will be felt more intensely by the other partner than a more modest-sized one, but by no means does this mean that a person with a smaller penis can't give pleasure to their partner.

The penis can experience breakdowns. Even if desire is present and strong, fatigue and stress may prevent an erection. If these breakdowns are frequent (called erectile problems), it could be a good idea to consult a health professional to determine the source of the problem, which could be biological, physiological or psychological.

Some men have a modest sexual appetite, and this doesn't make them less "masculine." Also, in the context of sexuality, emotions and psychology are usually associated with women, but men can and often do feel the need to combine emotions and sexuality.

* Circumcision is removal of the foreskin, the fold of skin that covers the glans of the penis. The reason that has long been given to justify performing this minor surgery on baby boys is that the glans is easier to clean without the foreskin. But circumcision isn't as common today as it used to be. In Canada the circumcision rate has been declining. It's around 32 percent and varies quite a bit between regions. The rate in Canada is similar to the global average. But in the United States the numbers are quite different—a 2016 study found that 71.2 percent of men are circumcised.

HOW LONG?

People often worry about the size of their penis, despite the fact that its size doesn't determine the sexual pleasure they can give and receive. The average size? It's 3.6 inches (9.1 centimeters) for the flaccid penis (at rest), and 5.2 inches (13.2 centimeters) when it's erect.

THE PENIS EXPOSED

There is a penis museum in Iceland. No joke! The Icelandic Phallological Museum (the first part of *phallological* is from the word *phallus*, meaning "erect penis") opened its doors in 1997 and displays hundreds of penises from different mammals. The 2012 documentary *The Final Member* tells the unique story of the museum and its quest to obtain *the* missing member: the human phallus!

AKA

"phallus, (male) member, (male) organ, sex, erection; *North American informal* pee-pee; *Irish informal* mickey; *humorous* lunch box; *vulgar slang* cock, dick, prick, knob, chopper, tool, equipment, dipstick, ding-a-ling, dong, (one-eyed) trouser snake, shaft, ramrod, root, boner, length, meat, pudding, pego, John Thomas, Johnson, machine, manhood, thing, winkle, middle leg, third leg, old man, joystick, pencil, pisser, prong, putz, rig, rod, Roger, stalk, stiffy, tonk, tube, weapon, yard; *British vulgar slang* willy, horn, how's your father, peter, plonker, todger; *Irish vulgar slang* langer; *North American vulgar slang* dork, pecker, weenie, wiener, schlong, whang, whanger; *technical* intromittent organ; *archaic* membrum virile, virile member, nerve, person, propagator, tarse, verge, pizzle; *archaic, vulgar slang* loom, needle, pillicock, pintle, runnion [etc.!]"

—From the *Oxford American Writer's Thesaurus*
(Oxford University Press, 2012, 2019)

Physical and Sexual Attraction

Physical: adjective, from Latin *physicalis*, "concerning nature"
Sexual: adjective, from Latin *sexualis*, "sexual"
Attraction: noun, from Latin *attractio*, "a drawing toward"

"Why am I attracted to a particular person?" Well, it could be because you have common interests and values. But sexual attraction is said to be multimodal, meaning that several elements play a role in activating it.

> **Symmetry**. It could be that people are usually more attracted to people with well-proportioned, well-balanced physical characteristics—a symmetrical face, for example. Why? Because symmetry is one of the guarantees of good DNA, and there-fore of a person who's likely to be in good health. But recent studies have shown that in fact things are less straightforward, and that asymmetry, having traits that don't mirror one another on both sides of your face, is normal and attractive too.

> **Pheromones**. These are a type of chemical, similar to **hormones**, that are detected conciously or unconciously by our sense of smell. Pheromones could perhaps trigger sexual arousal. However few studies show a direct and tangible link between phero-mones and sexual attraction.

> **Voice, smell and appearance of the face and body** contribute to physical attraction. But researchers believe that further studies are needed to find out what it is about them that makes them more or less attractive to others.

During adolescence, attractions change. This is normal, as it's a time of exploration.

During adolescence, attractions change. This is absolutely normal. Adolescence is a time of **exploration**, and you have to remain open and frank—first with yourself, to know what your body and your head are telling you about your desires, and then, if it feels safe for you, with others, to discover what might appeal to you in return.

If you don't feel attraction for anyone, don't panic—it may come later. Or, if you are asexual (see **asexuality**), it never comes at all, and that's okay.

Pleasure

Noun, from Old French *plaisir*, "pleasure, enjoyment"

A 2011 study carried out by scientists at McGill University in Montreal looked at the pleasure people experience listening to music. Their findings? The participants began to secrete dopamine, "a neurotransmitter used to enhance or reward more concrete pleasures associated with food, drug use or money," both *before* and *during* their music-listening sessions. Pleasure mostly takes place in the brain. Is it the same for sexual pleasure? Absolutely.

Having fun and feeling pleasure in your sex life is crucial (see **sex games**). When you engage in sex with someone, it's usually to give and obtain pleasure. Of course, other elements come into play when sharing a sexual relationship: love, desire, the need to relax, to be validated and appreciated, the search for sensations, and many other intimate and personal reasons. Pleasure, however, should always remain central in your sexual relations. Sex with pleasure represents a way to take ownership of your body and take care of yourself and others. It benefits both your body and your mind.

> Pleasure mostly takes place in the brain.

Polyamory

Noun, from prefix of Greek origin *poly-*, "many" + Latin *amor*, "love"

Polyamory is the practice of having more than one romantic relationship at a time. Being polyamorous means being able to love several people at the same time in a consensual context—everyone involved is aware of the situation. It can include sexual relationships with more than one person, but it's not about having sex with multiple partners at the same time. Polyamory can also include diverse gender expressions and sexual orientations.

Pornography

Noun, from Greek *pornographos*, "that writes about prostitutes"

Pornography is the depiction of erotic behavior to cause sexual excitement. It can be offered in videos, photos or immersive experiences (as in virtual reality) and features one or more people (**actors**, most of the time actors) performing sexual acts in order to arouse those watching them. Porn is a lucrative industry, generating close to $100 billion annually. Since the advent of the internet, it has had a huge influence on teenagers—the average age for seeing the first porn movie is now 11 years old.

Pornography can be seen as part of the process of sexual awakening, but be careful: it often doesn't reflect reality. It merely reflects the sexual fantasies of those who produce it. Certain scenarios are tinged with violence, misogyny* or racism, and more often than not, they offer a degrading depiction of women.

The first time you have sex is never going to be the way porn portrays it—a good thing, too, as imitating the performances of porn actors would almost certainly hurt and be unpleasant. Not to mention it could disturb your partner and make them feel like not having sex again.

It's perfectly normal to feel curious about porn, but you have to remain critical about what you see. Thankfully, while pornography has a reputation for misrepresenting what healthy sexuality looks like, there are more and more websites committed to safe, inclusive, body-positive messages that don't objectify women.

* Misogyny is hatred of or prejudice against women. It can lead to violent words and actions actions directed at them.

A DARING INITIATIVE

At the Boston University School of Public Health there's a course on pornography called "Understanding Pornography: A Public Health Perspective." Students discuss the impact of pornography on the public and whether or not it promotes violence against women. The course covers different types of pornography and explores the positive and negative aspects of watching it.

Premenstrual Syndrome (PMS)

Premenstrual: adjective, from prefix *pre-*, "before" + *menstrual*
(from Latin *menstrualis*, "monthly; concerning menstruation")
Syndrome: noun, from Latin *syndrome*, "group of symptoms"

"Are you having your period?"

How many people of the female sex have heard this sexist joke used in an attempt to explain their mood swings? Loads! PMS, or premenstrual syndrome, is both famous and mysterious. Blamed for all evils, PMS is often invoked to explain sadness or susceptibility, mistakes, lack of concentration and so on. But beyond the sexist jokes and questionable comments, know that PMS is for some people a very difficult thing to experience each month.

Many people experience pain, breast tenderness, bloating or headaches before or during their period, and "between a third and a half...have moderate or severe symptoms." A 2017 study in the Netherlands found that 3 percent of participants missed work during almost every period, and the average woman missed 8.9 days a year because of menstrual pain, also known as dysmenorrhea. Although experiencing painful cramps may be normal, it could also be a sign of a more serious problem, like **endometriosis**.

A British study calculated that menstrual pain "can be almost as intense as the pain felt when suffering a heart attack"! The American College of Obstetricians and Gynecologists' website explains that menstrual pain is caused by the release of natural body chemicals called prostaglandins, which are made in the lining of the **uterus**. Among other things, they cause the muscles of the uterus to contract painfully.

Pronouns

From Latin *pronomen* (*pro-* "for, in place of" + *nomen* "name")

Pronouns are gaining more and more significance. An increasing number of people identify themselves as nonbinary, trans, queer or genderfluid and do not necessarily recognize themselves in traditional masculine or feminine pronouns like *he* and *she*, *his* and *hers*, and *himself* and *herself*. Fortunately, alternatives exist that bypass some of the binary rules of traditional grammar and allow for more diversity.

They, *them*, *their* and *themself* have become popular **gender-neutral** singular pronouns in English. Other options include *ze* for the personal pronouns *he* or *she*, and *zir* for the possessives *his* or *hers*.

Using a person's chosen pronouns is simply a matter of respect.

Psychological Androgyny

Psychological: adjective, from Latin *psychologia*, "study of the human mind"
Androgyny: noun, from Greek *andros*, "male person," and *gunē*, "female person"

As the impressive international sales of the book *Men Are from Mars, Women Are from Venus* by John Gray have shown, the idea that the masculine is the antithesis (the opposite) of the feminine is deeply rooted in our society. Yet it isn't true!

In reality, there's no question that a woman can work in the construction industry, even if that sector is dominated by men (with whom we associate ability to do the physical side of the job). Or that a man can indulge in knitting, even though it's typically associated with the female sex (who are supposedly more "passive" and interested in calm and meditative activities). What all this means is that a psychologically androgynous person is able to exhibit what we think of as both masculine and feminine attributes, regardless of their **gender**.

According to research by Julie Rosenzweig and Dennis Dailey (1989), sexual satisfaction is higher in people who possess psychological androgyny. Such people also show "more flexibility in their intimate relationships." Greater fluidity in our behavior and thought processes results in increased happiness and, in the context of our romantic and sexual life, greater openness and a better ability to understand others. Possessing psychological androgyny can also increase empathy, which is the capacity to put yourself in the place of others and understand what they feel. Of course, these qualities aren't exclusive to people displaying psychological androgyny.

PICTURING PSYCHOLOGICAL ANDROGYNY

To understand the notion of equilibrium, think of a scale. If you stand on one side of the scale, the other side tilts—it cannot stand horizontally. Should you follow the logic of John Gray's popular book *Men Are from Mars, Women Are from Venus*, there would be no possible equilibrium between those identifying as men and those identifying as women. But several studies have shown that people who are psychologically at the center of the scale (also known as the gender continuum) are better balanced. That's what psychological androgyny is: being able to display emotions and behaviors and perform actions that are associated with both masculine and feminine attributes.

173

Puberty

Noun, from Latin *pubertas*, "sexual maturity"

Puberty is the name for the period of transition from childhood to **adolescence**. It causes two types of major changes, primary sexual characteristics and secondary sexual characteristics, which are the differences between females and males. Primary sexual characteristics are the changes that can't be seen and develop inside the body: the **reproductive system** and the sexual organs that activate and get the body ready to procreate.

Secondary sexual characteristics are the external changes happening outside the body, to hair, breasts, penis and testicles, etc.

While these changes are common to all teenagers (with some exceptions), they can happen at different rates. Each person is unique. Unless there are specific health issues that affect puberty, there's no need to worry about these changes. It can be overwhelming at times to witness all these transformations, but it's normal to see your body adapt to a new reality.

While these changes are common to all teenagers (with some exceptions), they can happen at different rates.

WHAT CHANGES

PRIMARY SEXUAL CHARACTERISTICS	Development of the female reproductive system (uterus, ovaries, etc.)	Development of the male reproductive system (testicles, penis, etc.)
SECONDARY SEXUAL CHARACTERISTICS	Activation of the ovaries and uterus Menarche (first period) Ovulation Estrogen secretion Breast development Body-hair growth (on the pubis and armpits) Pelvic enlargement Increase of fatty tissue (fat storage on the body) Growth spurt	Increased testicular size Thorarche (first ejaculation) Testosterone secretion Muscle development Body-hair growth (pubis, armpits and face) Voice change Shoulder enlargement Growth spurt

QUEER
QUESTIONING

RAPE CULTURE
REPRODUCTIVE SYSTEM
RESPECT

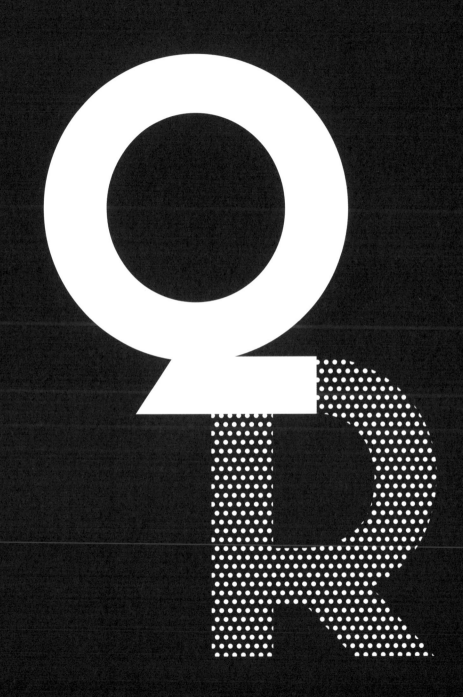

Queer

Adjective, possibly from German *quer*, "oblique, peculiar"

....

The first time the word *queer* was used to describe effeminate men was in 1894, in a letter written by John Douglas, 9th Marquess of Queensberry. In the letter he discusses his son, Lord Alfred Douglas, whose homosexuality and relationship with writer Oscar Wilde he had just discovered. He used the word as an insult.

Historically, *queer* meant "weird, odd, strange, peculiar, different, suspicious, ill…" And it was often used, as by Marquess Douglas, to discriminate against homosexuals, who were considered abnormal. In the 1980s the term was taken up and claimed by **LGBTQQIP2SAA+** groups, including Queer Nation, to make it the proud standard of a political struggle.

The ArQuives is an LGBTQQIP2SAA+ archive in Canada. It's one of the largest independent LGBTQQIP2SAA+ archives in the world. In 2020 the ArQuives published *Out North: An Archive of Queer Activism and Kinship in Canada* by Craig Jennex and Nisha Eswaran. For more information, go to arquives.ca.

Questioning

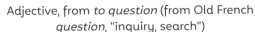

Adjective, from *to question* (from Old French *question*, "inquiry, search")

....

Representing one of the *Q*s in the initialism **LGBTQQIP2SAA+**, *questioning* is used to describe a person who hasn't made a final decision on their **sexual orientation** or gender **identity**. Some people will go through occasional periods of questioning, while others will remain questioning all their lives. Either way, sexual orientation and gender identity is a personal process that must be respected.

R

Rape Culture

Rape: noun, from Anglo-Norman French *rap*, "a seizing"
Culture: noun, from Middle French *culture*, "cultivation, culture"

Rape culture is talked about a lot in the media and on social networks. What is it exactly? Its meaning is simple enough. It's any gesture, word, decision or behavior that trivializes sexual assault. The word *culture* here does not refer to any artistic activity, but rather to a set of beliefs, practices and values that characterize a society.

Some examples:

> Saying to a person who's been raped that they "had it coming" or "were looking for it" because they wore sexy clothing. Many **sexual assaults** are never reported because the victims—mostly women but also, let's not forget, some men—feel they won't be believed and might even be blamed for what happened. (This is known as **victim blaming**, which is exactly what it sounds like: blaming the victim for the assault or harassment they've suffered.) In the United States in 2018, only 25 percent of rapes were reported to police. In Canada, only around 5 percent of sexual assaults are reported to police.

> Placing advertisements, whether in magazines, on billboards or on television, in which women are shown as sexual objects.

> Spreading the idea that men's sex drives are so hard to control that they need to satisfy them at all costs.

> Teaching/requiring girls to hide their bodies so as not to arouse the boys.

A short animated video called *James Is Dead* by Blue Seat Studios explains rape culture and victim blaming: youtu.be/Op14XhETfBw.

Reproductive System

Reproductive: adjective, from *to reproduce* (from prefix *re-* + Latin *producere*, "to generate," from *pro*, "forth," and *ducere*, "to bring forward")
System: noun, from Latin *systema*, "arrangement of parts"

....

The reproductive system is the biological and physiological system that contains all the elements necessary for reproduction (for the creation of a fetus). Biologically speaking, there are two systems, one female and one male.

On the female side, we find external organs (**vulva**) and internal organs (**vagina**, Bartholin's glands, **fallopian tubes**, **ovaries** and **uterus**).

On the male side, we also find external organs (**penis** and scrotum) and internal organs (urethra, **testes**, vas deferens and seminal glands like the prostate).

Respect

Noun, from Old French *respect*, "observance, consideration"

....

Respect is the foundation of everything else! When it comes to sexuality, we all want fun and pleasure, but what we want above all is to feel respected. Respect for our bodies, limits, desires, needs, identity, gender and sexual orientation is essential.

Respect is an element that must be part of any relationship with others. It's a human right, and feeling respected in your sexuality should never be optional.

S

Semen

Noun, from Latin *semen*, "seed"

Semen is the body fluid that comes out of the **penis** through the urethra during **ejaculation** and contains sperm.

Here's something important to know: Before ejaculation, the penis secretes what's called pre-ejaculatory fluid, or pre-cum, which some scientists believe may contain a small of spermatozoa. This is why, in the case of heterosexual sex, you should use a condom from the *beginning* of sex if you want to prevent unwanted pregnancy.

Semen carries sperm, but it can also transmit **STDs** or **STIs**. Remember that regardless of the type of sexual relations you're having, condoms are always an effective way to protect yourself.

HEAVY SEMEN

Internationally renowned American photographer Andres Serrano has repeatedly used sperm in his provocative works. *Semen and Blood III* (1990) was used as the cover of *Load*, heavy-metal band Metallica's sixth studio album.

Sex

Verb, from Latin *sexus*, "sex, gender"

Some people think of sex as "complete" only if it includes penetration, and penetration done by a man inserting his penis into a woman's vagina. But this is a heterocentric view (see **heterosexuality**) that doesn't represent everyone's sexuality. For example, does this mean that two lesbian women never have legitimate sex if no penetration takes place between them?

In fact, every sexual activity is sex, whether it includes penetration or not. What matters is feeling **pleasure**, being comfortable with the partner (or partners) you're sharing the experience with, and, above all, feeling respected.

Sex Games

Sex: noun, from Latin *sexus*, "sex, gender"
Game: noun, from Old English *gamen*, "sport, mirth, game"

One meaning of the word *game* is "a physical or mental activity, neither imposed nor strictly utilitarian, to which people devote themselves in order to feel pleasure and entertainment."

This definition contains crucial elements for understanding how beneficial it can be to integrate an element of play into your sexual activities.

First, a game involves both body and mind. Your body isn't only functional but is also endowed with thoughts and emotions, which can become part of the game.

Second, a game isn't imposed but freely accepted. You participate in a game of your own free will—no one is forcing you.

Finally, a game's sole purpose is to provide **pleasure** to its participants.

During your first sexual experiences, perceiving sex as a kind of game can help make you feel comfortable. But playing a game isn't about impersonating a character and becoming someone you're not. The goal is to experience pleasure, let go, establish intimacy with others and be confident enough to be completely yourself with your partner(s). You have to let go of all seriousness for a moment, allow yourself to laugh and embrace the freedom to explore.

Through play, sexual partners can get to know each other and develop agreeable, even funny interactions that allow them to relax and enjoy these moments which at first may have seemed stressful. And that also applies to *solitary* sexual games. Learn to relax and play with your own body as you would when having sex with another.

Some people will be totally at ease without integrating a notion of play into their sexual activities. Can you have a fulfilling sexual relationship without play entering the equation? Of course! The idea is for everyone to enjoy the moment with respect and trust.

Sex Positions and Practices

Sex: noun, from Latin *sexus*, "sex, gender"
Positions: plural of the noun, from Latin *positio*, "a putting, position"
Practices: plural of the noun, from Greek *praktikē*, "of or pertaining to actions"

There are a thousand and one ways to experience sex, and it's impossible to list all sexual positions here. But the following well-known practices give a glimpse of what's possible to explore and experience. And don't forget that each one of us is free to improvise further and improve upon existing models!

(See also **Kama Sutra**.)

Anal intercourse: When a penis is inserted into and held by the anus while partners move their bodies in ways that feel good to them (see **anal sex**).

Anilingus: Oral sex on the anus (see **anal sex**).

BDSM: Describes sexual play or relationships involving exchanges of power and pain. B = bondage, D = discipline or dominance, S = submission or sadism, M = masochism.

Blow job: See **fellatio** and **oral sex**.

Cybersex: Virtual (as in, not in person) sexual experiences or encounters that involve text conversations or visual exchanges via the internet.

Doggy style: Describes a position in which a person sits on their knees behind their partner and penetrates them with a penis or sex toy from behind. The name comes from the position taken by dogs when they're mating.

Dry sex: A kind of sex where people have clothes on but are pressing their genitals together for sexual pleasure. This can also be called *frottage*, *grinding* or *dry humping*.

Fingering: Penetration of the anus or vagina with fingers (see **masturbation**).

Fisting: A term used to describe deep manual sex, where many fingers or a hand are gradually inserted into the vagina or anus.

Glory hole: Popular in pornography, this is a hole made in a wall (often in one of the cubicles of a public toilet) through which a person inserts their penis to be masturbated, receive fellatio or penetrate an unknown person on the other side of the wall. A person with an anus or a vagina can sit against the glory hole and be penetrated, masturbated or given oral sex.

Golden shower: A person urinates on their partner or is urinated on by them for the purpose of sexual pleasure.

Hand job: Providing pleasure to someone's genitals with your hands (see **masturbation**).

Kink/kinky: Describes sexual practices or activities that a person or group of people considers to be outside the "norm" or a person who enjoys or pursues those practices.

Making out: A vague term that often refers to a session of extended activity that includes passionate or deep kissing, some kind of other body contact and perhaps other kinds of sex, like manual sex (fingering or hand jobs).

Manual sex: Sometimes called *digital sex*, this refers to using the hands and fingers to sexually stimulate the genitals or other parts of the body. Fingering, hand jobs or "fisting" (deep manual sex) are kinds of manual sex (see **masturbation, hand job, fisting**).

Missionary: A position in which one person lies on their back and the other one lies on top of them during sex.

Mutual masturbation: The practice of sexual partners masturbating together. Sometimes people use this term for manual sex (fingering or hand jobs) done at the same time (see **masturbation**).

Oral sex: The practice of using one's mouth and tongue on a partner's penis, clitoris or anus to give them pleasure. Also referred to as *going down on someone* or *giving head*.

Petting: Affectionate or sexual stroking and touching. Petting historically has also meant any kind of sex other than intercourse. When it includes genital sex, it's sometimes called *heavy petting*.

Phone sex: Sexual encounters or experiences in which people talk about sex or role-play sexually via the telephone, often paired with masturbation.

Queening (aka face-sitting or kinging): Sitting astride your partner's face to allow contact between the mouth and the genitals or anus. Queening is a practice found in BDSM.

Rim job: Sexual slang for performing oral sex on someone's anus (see **oral sex**).

Safer sex: Sexual practices that aim to reduce the risk of **STDs** and **STIs**, such as using condoms and other barriers, testing regularly for infections and limiting the number of sexual partners. It's the word *safer* instead of *safe* because these practices reduce risk greatly but cannot remove all risk.

Scissoring: A sexual position in which two partners sit facing each other and cross their legs so their genitals touch. Popular culture wrongly associates scissoring only with lesbian sex.

Sixty-nine (69): A sex position in which two people align themselves so that each person's mouth is near the other's genitals and simultaneously perform oral sex on the other (see **oral sex**).

Starfish: Describes sexual relations during which a person merely lies like a starfish, legs apart and arms outspread, with no movement but enjoying the affection of their sexual partner(s).

Tea-bagging: A slang term for a man placing his scrotum in the mouth of his sexual partner for sexual pleasure.

Threesome: A term to describe a sexual experience or relationship in which three people actively interact.

Tribadism (or tribbing): Rubbing one's genitals against another person's genitals directly, usually without clothing, to express sexual feelings and obtain sexual pleasure. Used most often in lesbian sex.

Vaginal intercourse: When a penis or sex toy is inserted into and held by the vagina while partners move their bodies in ways that feel good to them, either for sexual pleasure or to reproduce.

Sex Toys

Sex: noun, from Latin *sexus*, "sex, gender"
Toy: noun, from Middle English *toye*, "funny remark; piece of entertainment"

Exploring your body is important in order to discover your sexual tastes and preferences. And sexual **exploration** can be done alone, in pairs or in groups. It's also possible to incorporate sex toys that are designed for **pleasure** and fun. The most famous sex toys are probably the dildo, a sort of penis-shaped cylinder that's inserted into the mouth, vagina or anus, and the vibrator, which can be used on many parts of the body.

Several other objects are designed to enhance sexual **arousal** and make you feel good, stimulating, for example, the clitoris, the nipples, the **erogenous zones** of the anus and so on. There are also vaginal and anal stimulators, like the famous anal and vaginal beads (small spheres that can be inserted into the anus or vagina) and the anal plug, which, as its name makes clear, is inserted into the anus.

No matter what type of sex toy you decide to use, your desire to explore is the only thing that matters. The rest is up to your imagination. If it speaks to you and intrigues you, why not give it a try? On the contrary, if it leaves you indifferent, forget about it and move on.

EVER HEARD OF TELEDILDONICS?

Pleasuring yourself with a smartphone? Finally included in your plan! Several mobile apps today invite you to participate in erotic games or even make your partner have an orgasm thanks to a sex toy plugged into their smartphone. You may arouse your partner while being in a different room by remotely triggering a plugged-in sex toy (say, a vibrator). It's that crazy, and it's called teledildonics (funny name, eh?—the prefix of Greek origin *tele-* means "at a distance," as in "television" and "telescope"). But the concept of teledildonics isn't new and was invented in 1974 by the information technology pioneer and author Ted Nelson.

Sexism

Noun, from *sex* (from Latin *sexus*, "sex, gender") + the suffix
of Latin origin *-ism*, "prejudice, discrimination"

Sexism is **discrimination** against a person on the basis of their **gender**. More and more, there is talk of ordinary or microsexism, a type of sexism accepted and normalized by society. All sexism perpetuates problematic gender **stereotypes** that prevent people, especially children, from exploring certain domains, having formative and revealing experiences or developing specific interests and skills.

KNIGHTS AND PRINCESSES

Here's a perfect example of ordinary sexism. In 2017, at a day camp in Quebec, children were offered a knights-and-princesses-themed activity. They were divided into two groups. While the boys faced a dragon and took their seats at King Arthur's table, the girls dressed up as princesses and entered a beauty pageant where the jury was made up of...boys!

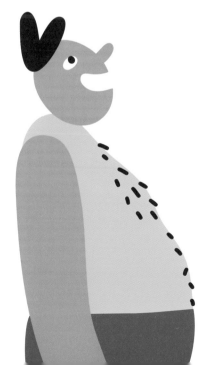

Sexting

Noun, a blend of *sex* (from Latin *sexus*, "sex, gender")
+ *(t)exting*, "sending a text message"

Your smartphone allows you to do many things—buy movie tickets, play games, jot down your appointments, chat with family, friends and acquaintances...and sext. Sexting is sending messages to flirt and seduce other people, which can be really fun and exciting. But you have to be careful what you send and who you send it to.

In an ideal world, you wouldn't send anything to anyone (including dick pics!), because you never know what other people might do with those photos and conversations, but we know people still do it. When sex texts, or sexts, aren't requested by the person you're conversing with, it's inappropriate and reprehensible to send them. Sending or receiving intimate photos is risky, but there are ways to protect yourself and practice **consent** even via text. For example, ask the person if they want to receive a naked image.

Since 2001 the Supreme Court of Canada has considered sexting legal in the following cases:

> the images are taken and sent by the senders themselves;

> the images are sent and received voluntarily between two consenting individuals of approximately the same age;

> the images contain no signs of violence or aggression;

> the images remain private and aren't shared on social networks or among a circle of friends.

The main goal of the law about sharing intimate images is to protect people from revenge porn.

In an ideal world, you wouldn't send anything to anyone (including dick pics!), because you never know what other people might do with those photos and conversations.

DICK PICS, OR HOW NOT TO SEXT

Dick pics (photos of penises received via text or chat) may be considered exhibitionism (undressing or showing your genitals in public) if they're unsolicited. Needless to say, few people enjoy receiving a photo of a penis out of the blue. Sending sexually explicit images can be a sexy game between two consenting people, but the unexpected arrival of a photo of an erect penis isn't a joke and can be a criminal offense in some cases.

Sexuality

Sexual: noun, "action or fact of being sexual," from Late Latin *sexualis*,
"relating to sex," + suffix *-ity*, from Latin *itatem*, "state or condition"

....

In 1981 Dennis Dailey, professor of social welfare at the University of Kansas, developed the Circles of Sexuality model. Aimed at future social workers, it set out to promote a positive, inclusive, diverse and healthy vision of sexuality. The model is based on a holistic (global) view of sexuality and includes five circles, each representing a value that intersects with its neighbors. The values are sensuality, intimacy, sexual identity, sexual and reproductive health, and sexualization.

These interacting dimensions influence or determine people's understanding of sexuality. For example, a person's issues with their body image will almost certainly affect the quality of their sex life. Someone struggling to be intimate with another person will probably find it difficult to explore their sexuality or even have a sex life at all. The goal of Dailey's model is, above all, to make people aware of the complex intersection of emotions, values and attitudes that defines us and shapes our perceptions of sexuality.

Sexual Assault

Sexual: adjective, from Latin *sexualis*, "concerning sex"
Assault: noun, from Old French *assault*, "an attack"

....

It's hard to talk about sexual assault, but that doesn't mean we shouldn't, especially in light of the rise of movements like **#MeToo** and #WhyIDidntReport. And while this book is intended to be the most inclusive and the least gendered of encyclopedias, statistics force us to tell it like it is:

> The vast majority (96 percent) of alleged perpetrators of sexual offenses are male. Of these, 75 percent are adult men and 25 percent are boys, while 84 percent of the victims are female.

> Sexual offenses are committed most frequently against girls between the ages of 12 and 14.

What is sexual assault?

Simply put:

> Sexual assault can take the form of a kiss, stroking, unwanted touching (a touch of the hand on a breast, buttock or the genitals, for example), masturbation or penetration.

> Sexual assault can occur without physical contact. *Voyeurism* is observing a person without their knowledge while they're naked or partially undressed, such as spying on another person while they're undressing in their room. *Exhibitionism* is someone showing their genitals to a stranger or taking photos of themself and sending them to other people.

> A sexual assault happens without the **consent** of the other person. The sexual abuser can use force, blackmail, manipulation or power to achieve their ends.

What is sexual violence?

Anyone can experience sexual violence, including children, teens, adults and elders. The people who commit the sexual abuse can be acquaintances, family members, trusted individuals or strangers.

The World Health Organization (WHO) defines sexual violence as: Any sexual act, attempt to obtain a sexual act, unwanted sexual comments or advances, or acts to traffic, or otherwise directed, against a person's sexuality using coercion,* by any person regardless of their relationship to the victim, in any setting, including but not limited to home and work.

Sexual violence is a reprehensible act punishable by law. It can affect anyone, regardless of age, sex, gender and sexual orientation. The WHO definition includes rape, **sexual harassment**, **cyberbullying** and **sexual assault**.

* Coercion means forcing someone to act against their will. Rape, for example, is a coercive act.

What is rape?

Rape is a type of sexual assault whereby sexual activity is obtained by force, threat or violence. It includes forced penetration of the vagina or anus with a penis, fingers or an object, and coerced fellatio or cunnilingus. Rape is never consensual.

Sadly, rape can affect anyone, regardless of age, sex, gender or sexual orientation. It's a very serious assault and is punishable by law.

Most of the time, rape is committed by someone close to the victim.

The majority of sexual assaults are committed by someone known to the victim. And that's what makes it all the more difficult to denounce. The common image of the stranger attacking in the night? That's a rare occurrence.

What should I do if I've been sexually assaulted?

The first thing to do is to talk to someone you trust. They can help you access supports, including how to make a statement to police. Your goal is to make a formal complaint as quickly as possible, not only to provide details they will need to pursue your attacker but also, and most important, so that medical personnel can collect physical evidence of the assault. They'll complete a forensic exam, which includes collecting saliva, semen and blood from you in order to find traces of the attacker's DNA. To be effective, this exam must be done within five days of the sexual assault.

THE WEIGHT OF RAPE

In 2014–2015, American activist and performer Emma Sulkowicz caused a stir around the world with *Mattress Performance (Carry That Weight)*. Sulkowicz was raped by a fellow student during her second year at Columbia University, and for a year after that she carried a dorm mattress (a metaphor for the rape scene) wherever she went to demand that the student who assaulted her be expelled.

ACTIONS WITH CONSEQUENCES

Rape with penetration is the most obvious form of sexual assault. But many other types of sexual assault, even though they might not be as overt, are violent and can have far-reaching consequences for victims. For example, forcing another person to watch pornography or to show their genitals are both serious acts, classified as assaults under the Criminal Code of Canada. They are punishable by law.

Unfortunately, most sexual assaults aren't reported to the police because victims often fear they won't be believed. It can also be extremely difficult for a person who has just been assaulted in this way to "relive" it all with a police officer. But there are organizations that help victims of sexual assault and support them in the process. Here are a few of them:

In Canada:
> Royal Canadian Mounted Police: rcmp-grc.gc.ca/en/relationship-violence/information-sexual-assault-survivors
> Canadian Resource Centre for Victims of Crime: crcvc.ca
> Assaulted Women's Helpline: awhl.org

In the United States:
> National Sexual Violence Resource Center: nsvrc.org

Being sexually assaulted is a serious and traumatic experience that may leave long-lasting mental, emotional or physical scars. If you're a victim of sexual assault, it's important to talk to someone you trust so you don't have to go through this alone.

What should I do if someone tells me they've been sexually assaulted?

There are simple ways to show your support and help them. First you must listen to them and, most important, say you believe them. Many victims fear they won't be taken seriously if they tell their story. By keeping the information to themselves, they live alone with the effects of trauma. So be sure to comfort them, don't make them feel guilty about what happened, and ensure they're no longer in any danger. Referring them to pertinent help centers is also a good idea.

Sexual Harassment

Sexual: adjective, from Latin *sexualis*, "concerning sex"
Harassment: noun, from the verb *to harass* (from French *harasser*, "to tire out")

Sexual harassment is the act of tormenting another person verbally or physically by making unwanted and inappropriate comments and gestures of a sexual nature.

It can take many forms—an insistent gaze, an inappropriate comment, a sexual joke, an allusion to the other's sex life, a sexual gesture, etc. Sexual harassment is typically experienced in public spaces, such as in the workplace or at school. Examples include:

> a classmate who inappropriately and repeatedly comments on the body of another student;
> a teacher who offers to give someone a higher grade for a test if they accept being touched in a sexual way;
> a student who texts unsolicited sexual images to another student;
> a boss who forces an employee to stay after hours, making advances to them and threatening loss of their job if they refuse.

These are all unacceptable behaviors that are punishable by law.

HOLLABACK!

The Hollaback! initiative and photoblog was launched in 2005 in New York to compile testimonials from people around the world who have experienced harassment. The phone app also geolocates the spots where the events occurred and shows the extent of sexual harassment. Check it out at ihollaback.org.

A REAL THREAT

In 2018 Statistics Canada reported that one in three women had experienced some form of unwanted sexual behavior in public—unwanted sexual attention, physical contact or comments about their sex or gender.

RECOGNIZE HARASSMENT

In April 2017 a social media campaign called #ThatsHarassment was launched to educate the public on the different forms that sexual harassment can take in the workplace. Six videos illustrated situations of sexual harassment experienced by women. The goal? To make it easier to recognize what sexual harassment looks like.

In a study by the nonprofit organization Stop Street Harassment, 37 percent of women reported not feeling safe walking home at night, and 65 percent of American women experienced street harassment.

In 2012, Flemish student Sofie Peeters used a hidden camera to film the street harassment she experienced on a daily basis in Brussels. In the short film that resulted from her experience, titled *Femme de la rue* ("Woman of the Street"), several men are heard harassing her and calling her "bitch" or "whore" for refusing or not responding to their advances. The film toured the world, highlighting the issue.

Street harassment involves insults, unsolicited questions and requests, intimidation, humiliation and threats. For example:

> a man is called "faggot" because he adopts attitudes and gestures considered "effeminate";

> a trans person is insulted because of who they are;

> you are followed by a passerby when you indicate you're not interested in starting a conversation with them.

In an ideal world, this type of behavior wouldn't exist, but since it does, you need to know how to protect yourself. Here are some tips for getting out of or avoiding a problematic situation:

> Enter an open store to ask for help and report the person or people following you.

> If you're on a bus, tell the driver about the situation and ask them to stop closer to your home or at a place where it's safer for you to get off.

> Use mobile apps created specifically to counter harassment. These offer remote support, a direct link to the police, the ability to record the sounds of the surroundings (making it possible to recognize the pursuer) or a geolocation tool so a trusted person can monitor your route and make sure you arrive safely at home.

Sexual Orientation

Sexual: adjective, from Latin *sexualis*, "concerning sex"
Orientation: noun, from Latin *orient*, "rising or east"

Meredith, like Tom, is attracted to girls. Patrick is attracted to boys, Judith to both girls and boys, and Carl says he's primarily interested in the person he's with rather than a particular gender. Meredith identifies as a **lesbian**, Tom as heterosexual (see **heterosexuality**), Patrick as homosexual (see **gay**), Judith as bisexual (see **bisexuality**) and Carl as pansexual (see **pansexuality**). Marie, by contrast, doesn't feel sexual attraction for anyone and identifies as **asexual**). But each one of these inclinations can change over time.

In short, sexual orientation is used to describe a person's typical emotional, sexual and romantic attraction to a particular sex, to both sexes or to all sexes and genders (or to none at all).

Slut-Shaming

Slut: noun, from Middle English *slutte*, "scruffy woman"
Shaming: noun, from *to shame* (from Old English *scamu*, "shame")

Slut-shaming is the practice of commenting on and/or harshly judging people (mostly female) who express their **sexuality** openly or have an active sex life. The goal of slut-shaming is to make the target person feel like they're inadequate, inappropriate and a "whore" (thereby also passing judgment on sex workers). It's a value judgment that can do a lot of harm. Slut-shaming has many negative affects on its victims: they may develop eating disorders, depression, anxiety, body dissatisfaction and even suicidal thoughts.

Generating shame, especially in women, isn't new—women have long been made to feel they should act and dress a certain way. The madonna–whore complex, a sexist dichotomy whereby women are seen either as "pure virgins" or "dirty whores," is, unfortunately, still very present in the collective mentality. Society still promotes the idea that women shouldn't be sexual beings, affected by desire, as that is somewhat frowned upon or considered wrong.

"The fantasy of purity, which demands that women not be spontaneously inclined toward sex, undermines their empowerment since they're thereby supposed to resist sex. They are forbidden to seek it in the time and manner in which they want it."

—Lili Boisvert, *Screwed: How Women Are Set Up to Fail at Sex* (2017)

Stereotypes

Noun, from French *stéréotype*, "printing mold" from Greek *stereos*, "solid," and *tupos*, "mark, character"

Even before we're born, our parents or care-givers choose a first name for us and create a universe on our behalf—a room decorated with care, toys selected according to what they know about us, which is not much: our **gender**, perhaps, if that isn't kept a mystery. From the very beginning, we're associated with one of two genders: girl or boy. In Western society, the feminine/masculine division is omnipresent and represents the norm for a majority of people. These stereotypes about our gender deter-mine several aspects of our lives: the clothes we'll wear, the toys we'll play with, the way others will talk about us, the expectations other people have for us and our future. And without our noticing it too much, our gender **identity** gets defined by external factors, despite ourselves.

Several external factors play a role in these stereotypes—children's toys, for example. Since the 1980s, unisex toys (aimed at both girls and boys) have grad-ually been replaced by gendered toys. The same model of bicycle, for example, is usually offered in pink for girls and in blue for boys. According to present social codes, a boy can't have a pink bicycle, nor a girl a blue bicycle! For the companies that manu-facture the bicycles, being able to sell two bicycles to the same family is obviously much more profitable.

"NO TEA, NO SHADE"*

In order to break gender stereotypes among children as early as possible, several libraries in the United States (in New York, San Francisco...) are offering the Drag Queen Story Hour.**

Drag queens are invited to come and read a story to the children. The goal of the event? To open new horizons to young readers, show them that there are multiple identities and expressions of gender, and teach them tolerance and respect for everyone's differences.

Drag Queen Story Hour is a program started by Michelle Tea and RADAR Productions in San Francisco in 2015. It offers literary programming for kids and teens with a global network of local organizations. Find out more at dragqueenstoryhour.org.

* Expression used in the drag community, inserted at the beginning of a sentence and meaning "No disrespect, but..."
** *Drag queens* are people who portray women or female characters; *drag kings* portray men or male characters. Using costumes and makeup that exaggerate their features, drag queens and kings portray celebrities or create original characters.

By thinking that men want to have sex much more often than women do, people stigmatize all men and women for whom that stereotype isn't true.

Gender stereotypes have an impact on many spheres of life, including **sexuality**. By thinking, for example, that men want to have sex much more often than women do, people stigmatize all men and women for whom that stereotype isn't true. Saying that boys are more dominating than girls in intimate relationships suggests that girls are more passive and usually wait for boys to seduce them. But that's false! Every human being is different, and what people like and how they experience their sexuality differs from person to person, going far beyond the fixed conceptions that force us to think in terms of boys/girls and men/women (see **psychological androgyny**).

Stress

Noun, from Middle French *estrece*, "narrowness"

Stress is a physical or psychological reaction to a situation you find unsettling. It can be felt in a variety of situations—a difficult school exam, your first meeting with someone you like, the first time you have sex, a conflict with a friend, an argument with your parents, etc. **Adolescence** can be particularly stressful because a lot of changes take place during this time.

You can overcome stress by making your environment a safe and healthy place, one in which you feel comfortable and in control. Say you discover that you feel stressed out and sleep badly when you play video games for long stretches of time. Try avoiding playing them in the evening before your bedtime and organize shorter game sessions aimed only at relaxation. School exams have become too stressful? Try a form of meditation or yoga to help you deal with them, and study ahead of time instead of waiting until the last minute.

But stress can also be a good thing! It allows you to think twice before acting or making a decision that could have a major impact on your life. It can even prepare you to face specific situations. For example, being stressed before a job interview can motivate you to prepare better for it and therefore perform better.

During your first sexual experiences, it's normal to feel nervous, since this is all very new to you. Stress in these occasions can actually be a good way to connect with your own self, listen to your gut feelings, establish healthy sexual boundaries and know how far you're ready to go.

STDs or STIs

STDs (sexually transmitted diseases) and STIs (sexually transmitted infections) are infections that are passed on through sexual intercourse, with or without penetration, as well as through blood and other bodily fluids. STDs and STIs can have serious consequences for your health and the health of your partners, including infertility.

You should always protect yourself during sex by using a **condom**. A **dental dam** can come in handy when having oral sex. Experts recommend that people under the age of 25 get tested for STDs or STIs if:

> they've had unprotected sex;
> they've shared material for injecting or inhaling drugs;
> they've been tattooed or pierced with non-sterile material.

This is especially important if:

> one of the people involved had a sexual relationship with a partner (or partners) whose sexual past is not known;
> one of the people involved had sex with someone who has an STD or STI;
> one of the people involved has symptoms that resemble those of an STD or STI.

You can get tested by your doctor and in clinics specializing in sexual health.

In most of the United States, you can get checked for an STD or STI without having your parents involved. In Canada you need your health card to get checked, but there are youth-friendly clinics that will allow you to get tested even if you don't have your card.

STDs AND STIs THAT CAN BE CURED:

> Chlamydia

Chlamydia is the most common STD or STI in people aged 15 to 24 (67 percent of STDs or STIs in females and 44 percent of those in males). Chlamydia bacteria are transmitted through oral, vaginal or anal sex, touching the genitals of partners or sharing sex toys. Transmission can occur without penetration or ejaculation. Symptoms, when present, are pain when urinating or having sex, or abnormal discharge from the vagina or penis. Unfortunately, many people who have chlamydia don't experience symptoms and often continue to have unprotected sex, unknowingly infecting their partners. If left untreated, a chlamydia infection can lead to infertility, chronic pain in the lower abdomen or testicles, and chronic infection of the prostate.

> Gonorrhea

Gonorrhea bacteria are transmitted during penetration (oral, vaginal or anal). This infection can cause pain when urinating (a tingling or burning) and also during sex. There is sometimes abnormal discharge from the penis or anus, and, in males, a sore throat. Caution: People of the female sex tend not to have symptoms. If left untreated, gonorrhea can lead to infertility, chronic pain in the lower abdomen and infection of the testicles.

> Lymphogranuloma venereum (LGV)

LGV is a bacterium of the chlamydia family that mostly affects males. The modes of transmission are identical to those of chlamydia. Indications include painful swelling of the glands, discharge of blood or pus from the anus, and flu-like symptoms. If left untreated, LGV can cause serious damage to the genitals or anus.

> Syphilis

Syphilis had practically disappeared during the 20th century, but it's now resurfacing. In the United States in 2017 and 2018, there were more than 115,000 cases of syphilis. The modes of transmission are identical to those of other bacteria (see *chlamydia* above), but you can also contract syphilis through direct contact with a lesion on the skin of the infected person. You need to be careful, because symptoms may not appear right away and may seem like the flu or look like a rash on the body. Untreated syphilis can have severe consequences on the brain, bones, liver and heart.

STDs and STIs THAT CANNOT ALWAYS BE CURED:

> Hepatitis

Hepatitis is an inflammation of the liver caused by different viruses. Hepatitis B and C are spread by having sex with an infected person or coming into contact with infected blood. Symptoms of hepatitis often don't show, but when they do, they include, but aren't limited to, fatigue, fever and stomach pain. All types of hepatitis can be treated, but not neccesarily cured.

> Herpes (genital)

Two known types of the herpes simplex virus (HSV) are classified as STDs or STIs. Type 1, or HSV-1, is found mainly in the mouth, where it causes cold sores on the lips, but it can also be found on the genitals. Type 2, or HSV-2, only occurs only on the genitals.

Herpes can be transmitted through kissing, having sex (vaginally or anally) or giving or receiving **oral sex** (**fellatio**, **cunnilingus**). It is very contagious. There's no cure for herpes, only drugs to relieve the pain and reduce the lesions that result from it.

> HIV/AIDS

The human immunodeficiency virus, or HIV, is a virus that affects the immune system. If it develops at a later stage, it can cause AIDS (acquired immune deficiency syndrome). HIV can be transmitted through unprotected anal or vaginal sex and through blood (by sharing preparation, injection and inhalation drug equipment, or through tattooing and piercing with unsterile equipment). But HIV is *not* transmitted through everyday activities like shaking hands or kissing someone on the cheek. HIV doesn't discriminate and can affect anyone, regardless of gender and sexual orientation. At the moment there is no vaccine or cure for HIV. However, there are treatments that can control the virus and give people living with HIV a life expectancy comparable to that of the general population. HIV treatments can also be given to people at high risk of contracting the virus as a method of prevention (called prophylaxis or PrEP).

> Human papillomavirus (HPV)

The human papillomavirus (HPV) family is composed of several virus types, more than 40 of which can be sexually transmitted. These can be divided into two main categories:

> HPVs with a low risk of cancer, some of which cause condyloma (small warts on the genitals and sometimes in the throat);

> high-risk HPVs, which can cause cancer (of the cervix or anus).

HPV is spread during oral, vaginal or anal sex, or simply through contact between the genitals. It's the most common STD or STI in the world. There is a vaccine (free in certain regions). Routine use of condoms and dental dams is an effective way to protect yourself against HPV and other viruses.

For more info on contraceptives and sexual protection, go to the Centers for Disease Control and Prevention: cdc.gov/reproductivehealth/contraception/index.htm.

STDs or STIs CAUSED BY PARASITES:

> Pubic lice (crabs)

This is a species of lice that settles on the pubic hair surrounding genitals, causing itching and leaving small bite marks. You can get public lice through sexual activity or any kind of close contact with someone who has them. You can also get them by sharing clothing, bedding or towels with an infected person. It's essential to treat crabs, or they will continue to lay eggs and settle more and more comfortably on and around the genitals. Medicated creams and lotions to treat them can be bought over the counter or prescribed by a doctor.

Suicide

Noun, from Latin *suicida*, "act of suicide," from *sui*, "of oneself," and *caedere*, "to kill"

In adolescence, as in adulthood, life comes with its share of challenges, and there can be times when it's difficult to keep your head above water. Sometimes life feels so painful that there seems to be no way out, and you feel like giving up. At such times the act of suicide may seem like a solution—an extreme one. A sign of neither courage nor cowardice, suicide is, in fact, an act of despair.

The causes of depression, **stress** and **anxiety** are diverse and personal. Excessive drug and alcohol use (addiction), family problems, romantic breakups and questions relating to identity, gender and sexual orientation can cause life to turn upside down. Fortunately, *there's always hope*: each of these problems has potential solutions. What's important is to talk about it and get help.

LIGHT AT THE END OF THE TUNNEL

If you're having dark or suicidal thoughts, or if you see them in another person, it's very important to tell someone you trust and not keep it to yourself. Where can you get help?

Crisis Services Canada
crisisservicescanada.ca/en
1-833-456-4566

National Suicide Prevention Lifeline
suicidepreventionlifeline.org
1-800-273-8255

Kids Help Phone
kidshelpphone.ca
1-800-668-6868

TABOO
TAMPON
TESTES
TOXIC SHOCK SYNDROME
TRANSGENDER (PERSON)
TWO SPIRIT

Taboo

Noun, from Tongan *tabu*, "forbidden"

Strangely, even though we live in a hypersexualized society, many aspects of **sexuality** remain taboo.

COMMON TABOOS

Masturbation

Few people feel comfortable discussing masturbation in front of colleagues at work or in class. Even among friends, it's a subject that's often avoided. And yet most people masturbate! Masturbation is normal and healthy. In 2013 the World Health Organization published a report on sex-education standards in Europe in which it recommended educating children between the ages of four and six about masturbation and about discovering and enjoying their own bodies.

Periods

For a long time people didn't talk openly about periods either, and many women still hide their personal hygiene products in a pocket or in their hands when running to the bathroom to change them. Even though **menstruation** affects half of the planet's population, it's still difficult sometimes to broach the subject. According to a recent study in the United States, commissioned by a period-underwear company, 58 percent of the 1,500 women surveyed felt shame when menstruating!

The female sex

We've only just started to highlight the fact that the **clitoris** can reach a length of 4 to 6 inches (10 to 15 centimeters) and to value its sole purpose—**pleasure**! This isn't trivial. Modern textbooks usually illustrate it adequately, but until very recently the **clitoris** was represented as simply a tiny bit of pink flesh (if it was represented at all).

Violence experienced by men

Statistics about **sexual harassment** are alarming, and its victims are predominantly women. However, the majority of assaults go unreported, including those experienced by men, who may not speak out for fear of being judged for their distress, not being believed or being teased, all because of **stereotypes** that expect men to be strong at all times and able to defend themselves.

Virginity

Nowadays few people boast of being virgins (see **virginity**). But barely 60 years ago the norm was to wait until you were married before having sex with your partner. Young girls were told their virginity was "the most beautiful gift" to offer their husbands. Today people claim to have had sex multiple times in order to fit in and avoid being singled out and ridiculed. There's nothing embarrassing about being a virgin. Whether you have sex for the first time at 15 or 50 (or never!), you should be the only person judging what's right for you. Each person should be free to decide whether to have sexual relations and at what moment in their life. And it's okay to ask for help if the topic of your first sexual experience brings out feelings of anxiety or pain (because of low self-esteem, health problems, fears, trauma, etc.).

Anal sex

As you read earlier in this encyclopedia, the desire for anal penetration in men is often associated with being gay. Yet there's no direct correlation. A gay man might dislike anal sex altogether, and a straight man might love it.

And just because female pornographic actors have anal sex all the time doesn't mean it's openly discussed in the general population. Women still don't talk about it, even as anal sex becomes more and more common. In a 2014 study in Britain, almost one in five young adults reported having had anal sex.

Breaking down myths and taboos so that everyone is free to discuss sexuality adequately is everyone's responsibility. Sexuality is too important a topic in life to be avoided or repressed because of embarrassment or shame.

Tampon

Noun, from French *tampon*, "tampon," from Old French *tapon*, "plug made of cloth"

A tampon is a small, absorbent roll, with parts most often made out of cotton, rayon or polyester but also from polyethylene and polypropylene. It's inserted in the vagina during menstruation. The menstrual flow is absorbed by the material, preventing direct contact with the menstrual blood except when changing the tampon, which should be done every four to six hours. Changing your tampon regularly is important to avoid **toxic shock syndrome**. Health Canada requires that tampon companies indicate on the packaging the list of materials used in their products, as well as information on TSS, since the synthetic fibers contained in tampons may be involved in triggering the syndrome.

Some tampons come with an applicator to simplify insertion into the vagina. Others don't, in which case the tampon is inserted in the vagina using your fingers. What's the difference? The applicator makes it easier, because you don't have to put your finger in your vagina to insert the tampon, although in some brands it results in the use of more plastic. Tampons without an applicator and those with a cardboard applicator are eco-friendly choices. In the end, the method you choose to insert your tampon is up to you.

Tampons without an applicator and those with a cardboard applicator are eco-friendly choices.

GO RETRO!

Wearing a tampon allows you to go on with all your activities, including swimming. But if tampons today are considered practical, even liberating, it wasn't always the case.

When the first tampons with applicators were released in 1936, the public was reluctant to use them for religious and moral reasons. Was it erotic to insert something there? A young woman might tear her **hymen**!

Things have obviously evolved since then, but in the 1970s and early 1980s cases of toxic shock syndrome (TSS) were linked to tampon use. Today, the average for TSS cases related to tampon use is about 1 case per 100,000 people annually. It's always important to practice good hygiene and regularly change your tampon every four to six hours.

Testes

Noun, from Latin *testis*, "a witness (to virility)"

Testes are part of the male **reproductive system**. They are two round glands located inside the scrotum, which is a small bag of skin under the **penis** that maintains an ideal temperature for the testes to produce the sperm that is evacuated during **ejaculation**.

The testes are sensitive — consider the universal fear of the infamous and painful kick in the balls! — and thus an interesting **erogenous zone** to explore. Several sensations can be dramatically increased by playing with this region. You may sometimes worry about one of your testicles being larger than the other, but just as female breasts are never exactly the same, testicles of different sizes are completely normal.

Some people shave their scrotum. Motivations differ, but some claim that sensations are more vivid without hairs. That's ultimately up to you. Hairs can activate your sensory receptors and bring you *more* sensations (see **body hair**). Body hair or not, it's your choice!

SELF-TEST

Testicular cancer is the most common type of cancer in men aged 15 to 44, according to the Testicular Cancer Awareness Foundation. Self-testing frequently is the best way to spot an abnormality early. The foundation recommends you do it about once a month.

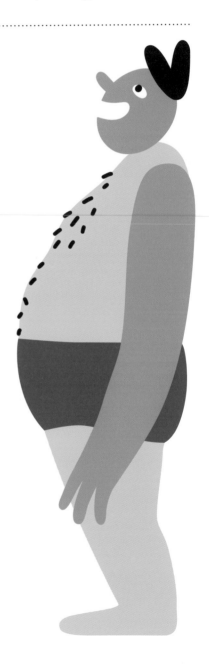

Toxic Shock Syndrome (TSS)

Toxic: adjective, from French *toxique*, "toxic, poisonous"
Shock: noun, from Middle French *choc*, "an attack or blow"
Syndrome: noun, from Latin *syndrome*, "group of symptoms"

....

Toxic shock syndrome (TSS) is an infection caused by bacteria that are already naturally present in the bodies of 20 to 30 percent of women. **Tampon** use is one way to trigger it.

The part of the tampon that absorbs blood during **menstruation** adheres directly to the vaginal mucosa. The tampon can therefore become a real bacterial "nest" that can result in an infection if it's kept in too long. To avoid this, use the right size tampon with the lowest absorbency and make sure you change your tampon every four to six hours and never keep it in longer than eight hours.

TOXIC TAMPONS

In 2012, fashion model and basketball player Lauren Wasser one day noticed the first symptoms of a hefty flu and wasn't feeling well. As she was also getting her period, she went out to buy some tampons. Several hours later she collapsed on the floor of her room.

At the hospital she learned that she had developed toxic shock syndrome, probably caused by a tampon worn too long. She narrowly escaped death, and both of her legs eventually had to be amputated.

Wasser's TSS was most likely caused by the chemicals in the tampon. Today, even after undergoing two amputations, Wasser is still modeling, playing basketball and lecturing extensively around the world to raise awareness of the potentially toxic products used in tampons.

Transgender
(Person)

Trans: adjective, from Latin *trans*, "across"
Gender: noun, from Old French *gendre*, "a kind, sort, category"
Person: noun, from Old French *persone*, "individual"

The word *trans* (as in *transgender* and *trans-identity*) is used to describe people who don't identify with the biological sex assigned to them at birth. It also refers to people who prefer not to be associated with a particular **gender**, male or female. A trans woman is someone who's born with a male gender but identifies with the female gender. A trans man is someone who's born female but identifies with the male gender.

Many trans people choose to change their appearance—through clothing, makeup, jewelry, hair removal or hair growth and so on. To match the gender they identify with, some trans people turn to **gender-affirming surgery** to alter their physical appearance including their genitals. This is called bottom surgery. But a trans person can also decide not to transition, not have an operation and not to undergo transgender hormone therapy. Each person follows their own path.

When talking about trans people, it's better to use the full term, *a trans person* or *trans people*, rather than just *a trans*, as the latter term dehumanizes trans people and adds to an already existing stigma. In addition, the term *transsexual* is now being abandoned in favor of *transgender*.

Transphobia is dislike of or prejudice against trans, nonbinary or gender-nonconforming people. It can take the form of rejection, insults, exclusion from the family unit, dismissal and so on. Transphobia can go as far as violent words and actions like harassment, sexual assault and even murder. Trans women are particularly targeted by transphobic violence (called transmisogyny).

A 2019 report on the National Transgender Discrimination Survey found that there has been a significant increase in harassment and violence against transgender people in the United States. Some 60 percent of those questioned had been physically assaulted, and 64 percent had experienced sexual assault.

Two Spirit

Adjective, translated from the Anishinaabemowin expression *niizh manidoowag*, "two spirits"

....

Two Spirit is a term that was introduced in 1990 by Elder Myra Laramee at the third annual Intertribal Native American, First Nations, Gay and Lesbian American Conference in Winnipeg. It reflects Indigenous Peoples' understanding of **gender expression** and identity. **Nonbinary** gender roles held a special place in precontact Indigenous communities. Once European settlers colonized Indigenous lands, they enforced the gender binary, and anyone not fitting into this classification was targeted. How each Indigenous nation defines genders varies from nation to nation.

Melissa Mollen Dupuis, an Innu columnist and Idle No More activist, explains that although "patriarchy and religions have imposed fixed identities and have banned multiple and fluid identities, [these] all have their place."

Many Indigenous artists, like the Anishinaabe musician Melody McKiver and Néhinaw artist Kent Monkman, are Two Spirit. Oji-Cree poet and novelist Joshua Whitehead also identifies as Two Spirit.

Non-Indigenous people identifying as Two Spirit are criticized and debated within Indigenous communities, but Mollen Dupuis argues that "[Two Spirit identity] means you understand and integrate the identity of everyone...without excluding anyone." That being said, if you use this word to describe your identity, it's essential to understand its meaning, its historical origin and its importance in Indigenous communities.

UNWANTED PREGNANCY

UTERUS

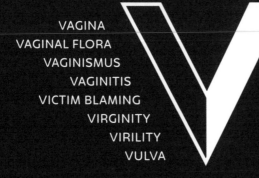

VAGINA

VAGINAL FLORA

VAGINISMUS

VAGINITIS

VICTIM BLAMING

VIRGINITY

VIRILITY

VULVA

X

Y

Z

U

Unwanted Pregnancy

Unwanted: adjective, from Old English prefix *un*, "not,"
+ verb, from Old Norse *vanta*, which eventually came
to mean "desire, wish for, feel the need of"
Pregnancy: noun, from Latin *praegnantem*, "with child"

When a fertile person with a uterus and a fertile person with a penis have sexual intercourse, there's always a risk of unwanted pregnancy (see **fertility**). Unintentional pregnancies can occur if the couple didn't use a contraceptive method during sex or used a **condom** that broke or was already punctured.

When an unwanted pregnancy occurs, many people turn to abortion. However, an unwanted pregnancy doesn't always end in an abortion, and an abortion isn't always the result of an unwanted pregnancy.

What is abortion?

We often forget it, but in North America abortion (also called voluntary interruption of pregnancy, or VIP) has been a right for only a few decades. The section of the Canadian Criminal Code that criminalized abortion was declared unconstitutional in 1988. That means abortion is legal in Canada. In the United States, abortion is a controversial and political issue, but it is legal everywhere except Alabama. That state recently banned all abortions except in cases where the mother's life is at risk. In many countries, abortion is punishable by law. In Honduras, for example, you can go to prison for eight years for having an abortion.

In Canada, abortion is available free of charge through medicare. If you're under the age of 12, you need permission from your parents or guardian to undergo an abortion. In the United States, most abortions are not covered by Medicaid, unless continuing the pregnancy will endanger the patient's life or if the pregnancy is a result of rape or incest. Thirty-seven states require parental consent for people under 18.

There are two main ways to terminate a pregnancy. The method used depends on the stage of pregnancy, meaning the number of weeks that have passed since fertilization. Pregnancy is usually calculated by trimester (by period of three months).

> Medication abortion, or abortion pill. This medication can be taken until the ninth week of pregnancy only, meaning during the first trimester. The procedure involves taking two tablets a few days apart, the first to interrupt pregnancy, the second to cause the egg to expel through contractions.
> Dilation and curettage. It's a minor surgical intervention, which is performed across North America at 12 weeks, the second trimester of pregnancy. The doctor inserts a small rod into the vagina to reach the uterus. A type of thin straw acts like a vacuum cleaner and removes any fertilized egg.

The majority of abortions in Canada and the United States are performed during the first trimester, between weeks 1 and 12. If the abortion procedure doesn't work and the fertilized egg is still clinging to the uterine wall even after curettage, the procedure must be repeated. Abortions are legal throughout an entire pregnancy in Canada. In the United States, some states have passed laws to ban abortions after a certain period of time—anywhere from 6 weeks in Alabama to 24 weeks in New York. For medical reasons, there are special exceptions made for abortions after 24 weeks.

ONE STEP FORWARD, TWO STEPS BACK

Since 2017, the abortion pill has been available to anyone in Canada wishing to terminate a pregnancy at nine weeks or less. In the United States the pill can cost upwards of $1,000, although it may often be less depending on where the abortion is performed and whether the patient has health insurance.

Choosing to have an abortion isn't an easy decision. People often have mixed feelings about it—fear, regret (or fear of having regrets), relief, worry, stress, anxiety and so on. Talk to someone you trust and who will help you make an informed decision you feel comfortable with. Your partner can, of course, be involved in the reflection and process, but the fact remains that it's up to you to decide whether to continue with your pregnancy. It's your body, after all!

The best way to prevent an unwanted pregnancy is to use **contraception** and **condoms**. They take away most of the stress!

Whether to continue with the pregnancy is up to you. It's your body.

Uterus

Noun, from Latin *uterus*, "womb"

....

The uterus is part of the female **reproductive system** and is located in the lower abdomen. It's about 3 inches (7 centimeters) long by 2 inches (5 centimeters) wide and during pregnancy can reach a diameter of up to 12 inches (30 centimeters).

At the lower part of the uterus is the cervix, which opens into the **vagina**. The uterus nourishes and houses the egg if fertilization occurs. If there's no fertilization, the uterus sheds its inner lining (endometrium) of blood and mucosal tissue (menses) through the vagina. Sperm pass through the uterus on their way to fertilize the egg.

The uterus is about 3 inches (7 centimeters) long by 2 inches (5 centimeters) wide.

225

Vagina

Noun, from Latin *vagina*, "sheath"

....

" 'Vagina.' There, I've said it...I say it because I believe that what we don't say we don't see, acknowledge, or remember. What we don't say becomes a secret, and secrets often create shame and fear and myths. I say it because I want to someday feel comfortable saying it, and not ashamed and guilty."

—From Eve Ensler's *The Vagina Monologues* (1996)

The vagina is an internal part of the female sex. The **vulva** and the vagina are often confused, although the two have very different functions. The vagina is a long muscle, located behind the vulva and connected to the cervix. It stretches during sexual **arousal** to facilitate penetration.

VAGINAS AT THE MUSEUM

There's a Vagina Museum in London! It organized its first exhibition in summer 2017 and is scheduled to become a permanent museum by 2032. See vaginamuseum.co.uk.

WATCH

Journalist and producer Liz Plank made a short documentary, *Divided States of Hygiene*, about the vagina's so-called dirtiness. (Spoiler: You guessed it—the vagina is *not* dirty!)

FISHY SMELL

Let's end this other myth. No, vaginas aren't dirty. The vagina doesn't need to be cleaned by you. It already contains all the elements needed to maintain the stability of its microbiota (see **vaginal flora**) and the correct level of acidity (pH), which ensure proper functioning and avoidance of infections such as **vaginitis**. Washing can disturb that balance.

So why are vagina-cleansing products sold? Because the myth of the smelly, mucky vagina is enduring.

Vaginas do have an odor, though, which is normal given the fact they're located inside the body, in a humid and warm place where (good) bacteria can proliferate. But it's a scent that isn't disgusting at all and doesn't "smell like fish," as many bad jokes claim. If your vagina *does* smell strongly of the seaside, something might be wrong and you should see a doctor or gynecologist!

Vaginal Flora

Vaginal: adjective, from Latin *vagina*, "sheath"
Flora: noun, from Latin *Flora*, goddess of flowers

Gut flora has generated a lot of interest in recent years following the discovery that our intestines are filled with billions of small bacteria, many of them useful for our health. Our gut has even been characterized as a second brain! More good news: the **vagina** also houses its share of extraordinary bacteria. They are collectively known as the vaginal flora, or vaginal microbiota.

Vaginal bacteria (lactobacilli) were called flora because at the time of their discovery (in 1892 by Albert Döderlein), scientists placed bacteria in the plant kingdom. In modern taxonomy, they occupy their own domain alongside eukaryotes and archaea.

Bacteria found in the vagina work hard to maintain a stable acidity level (pH), thereby preventing the appearance and development of germs. A change in the pH of the vaginal flora can lead to **vaginitis**.

In short, the vaginal flora or microbiota protect the vagina from infection and ensure the health of the female **reproductive system**. Thanks to it, you don't need to wash your vagina. It cleans itself (with the help of a few billion of its bacteria friends). No vaginal douches needed!

HOMEMADE YOGURT

While making your own yogurt is pretty trendy these days, using the bacteria in your vagina as a yeast starter is a rarer technique! But that's exactly what Cecilia Westbrook, a PhD student at the University of Wisconsin, tried—and succeeded!—in doing.

Vaginismus

Noun, from *vagina* (from Latin *vagina*, "sheath") +
the suffix of Latin origin -*ismus*, "condition"

Vaginismus is an involuntary contraction of the muscles of the pelvic floor that makes it difficult or impossible to have sex with vaginal penetration (whether with a penis, finger or sex object), insert a tampon during menstruation or even have a gynecological exam.

People with vaginismus don't know why their pelvic, perineal and vaginal muscles contract during penetration, and unfortunately the stress and anxiety this causes intensifies the physical reaction. People with vaginismus may have a strong desire for penetration but simply can't tolerate it.

Vicious circle

Several things can cause vaginismus, such as fear of penetration, a feeling that the penis—in the case of heterosexual sex—will be too big for the space of the vagina, vaginal dryness, a history of sexual assault and fear of getting pregnant.

Vaginismus can also be due to dyspareunia, which is the presence of pain during sex. Affected people begin to associate penetration with pain and develop fears that generate or worsen the muscle spasms.

In addition, vulvodynia, which is chronic pain in the vulva, can be caused by vaginismus, leading to a generalized fear of being touched in that region. Conversely, vulvodynia can lead to vaginismus.

Vaginitis

Noun, from *vagina* (from Latin *vagina*, "sheath") + the suffix of Latin origin -*itis*, "inflammatory disease"

....

Vaginitis is a word for various disorders that cause inflammation or infection of (you guessed it!) the **vagina**. Vaginitis can be caused by:
> a fungus;
> bacteria;
> trichomoniasis,* which can be transmitted through sexual contact.

Vaginitis can cause some itching or odors. It is *not* an STD or STI.

If you think you have vaginitis or have symptoms that resemble it (pain when going to the toilet, redness, odors, etc.), consult a doctor or other qualified healthcare professional (such as a gynecologist or school nurse) to get a correct diagnosis and rule out an STD or STI or other health problem.

Using condoms during sex is a good way to protect yourself from trichomoniasis which can cause vaginitis. On a daily basis, practice good hygiene (avoiding soap or using a pH-neutral soap, rinsing the genitals with water while taking a shower or bath) and wear clothing or underwear that isn't too tight.

---

* Trichomoniasis is an STI. It's caused by a parasite (a small living organism) and is usually contracted during sex via vaginal or urethral secretions. More rarely, trichomoniasis can be contracted via an object that contains or carries moisture, such as a toilet seat or a used towel.

Victim Blaming

Victim: noun, from Latin *victima*, "sacrificed animal or person"
Blaming: noun, from *to blame* (from Old French *blamer*, "to blame")

According to *Psychology Today*, victim blaming could be a normal human reaction—people are afraid that they'll be sexually assaulted, so they tell themselves that had *they* been in the victim's shoes, they would have acted or spoken in a way that prevented the assault. This way of thinking reassures them by letting them believe they're immune to sexual assault. But unfortunately, this isn't the case. And the victim remains blamed. This behavior is also witnessed in the context of **rape culture**.

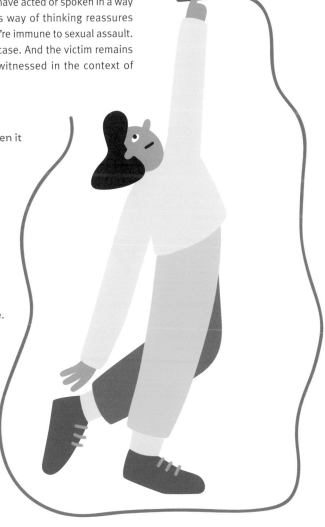

> "How were you dressed when it happened?"

> "Did you make it clear you didn't want to?"

> "Did you say no?"

> "Had you been drinking?"

These are the kinds of questions a victim of sexual assault may be asked when they speak out about a crime. They all imply that the assault may have been the victim's fault.

Virginity

Noun, from Old French *virginite*, "virginity," from Latin *virginitas*, "maidenhood"

....

Virginity means never having had sex. We often hear the expression "to lose your virginity." That's because for a long time people thought that having your first sexual encounter—especially for women—meant the "loss" of something—loss of innocence, loss of childhood, but also loss of a precious and unique element, virginity being associated with the idea of purity. Not being a virgin was considered dirty and was frowned upon. This kind of discourse, first used in a religious context and then becoming widely accepted, has long been used to convince young girls to wait as long as possible before having sexual intercourse for the first time—ideally, until they're married.

For young girls, loss of virginity is still associated with the tearing of the **hymen**. Which begs the question: How, then, do you assess a young lesbian woman's virginity if she won't be having sex with a man? What about men's virginity? Do they lose it when performing their first penetration? What about fellatio? What about masturbation? Is loss of virginity only an issue when there's vaginal penetration? What about young men having sex together? All in all, does virginity, and the "loss" of it, really matter? It's a personal question whose answer will vary greatly from one person to another.

Virility

Noun, from Middle French *virilité*, "virility," from Latin *virilitas*, "manhood"

....

Today virility encompasses all the characteristics of manliness—and in this book, by *man* we mean a person of the male sex. These characteristics include things like physical strength, courage, energy, warlike heroism, taste for domination, ability to reproduce and so on. They became considered male

attributes thousands of years ago, at the end of the Neolithic Age (no joke!). At this time, many human populations became sedentary, and as a result, social structures started to change: men became providers for the family, while women cared for the household and children.

These characteristics include things like physical strength, courage, energy, warlike heroism, taste for domination, ability to reproduce and so on.

Many people expect a man to be virile, regardless of the fact that virility is a cultural and social construction based on male/female roles that aren't reflected in real life or in the diversity of individuals and genders. The concept of virility comes with its share of questions. Are you less of a man if you're not virile? Since the capacity to procreate goes hand in hand with the definition of virility, how are we to characterize sterile men who can't have children?

Let's think about it some more. Does virility mean that a courageous, strong or domineering woman is "manly," and therefore a man? Obviously the answer is no.

There's a tendency to define masculinity and femininity according to physical criteria and preconceived and stereotypical images (see **stereotypes**). But there are countless ways to experience your masculinity or femininity and nothing preventing you from drawing from each of these two dimensions.

A recent study done by the American Psychological Association characterized "traditional" masculinity, involving "dominance and aggressivity," as harmful. The study even offers a practical guide to broaching the subject with boys and men. And in its first chapter, it states that "masculinities are constructed on social, cultural and contextual norms."

Vulva

Noun, from Latin *vulva*, "female sexual organ"

Some people don't know the difference between the **vagina** and the vulva, and that's because of the enduring **taboos** around the female sex.

The vulva is the name given to all the genitals outside the woman's body, those that can be seen and touched: the pubis (the small bump just before the beginning of the labia), the **clitoris**, the outer and inner lips (labia majora and labia minora) and the vaginal opening. The vulva also includes the Bartholin's glands (hidden behind the labia), the perineum and the urethra.

THANKS

Thank you, Pascal, for your ever-wise advice, for your ever-comforting presence, for all the sweetness that you bring to me, for our beautiful life.

Thank you to Emilie for believing in this project and for helping me "pitch" it to Éditions Cardinal. All of this would never have happened if we hadn't started that conversation about periods with Marianne and Matthieu. (Isn't it crazy that this book now exists?!)

Thank you to Aurore, my understanding and enthusiastic editor, who challenged me just enough and allowed me to better summarize my thinking and better manage my feelings of impostor syndrome.

A huge thank-you to Anne Vassal and Dr. Réjean Thomas for their proofreading and very relevant remarks.

Thank you, Estelle Cazelais, for your overwhelming encouragement and enthusiasm from the very beginning of this crazy project, for your super-relevant comments and all the work you do to make sexology fun, funny and cool. You rock!

Thank you to Isabelle Boisvert, an inspiring teacher who confirmed to me that I was on the right track in studying sexology, who showed me that you can talk about sexuality to young people in an intelligent and uninhibited way, with both passion and rigor. Your eagle eye has allowed me to take this book to the next level.

Thank you to Laurence and Anne-Marie, brilliant and sensitive friends whom I love so much.

Thank you, my beautiful Anne, for taking the time to read everything and comment with the usual enthusiasm and energy that make you the unique person you are. Thank you for always believing in the projects I take on (and for believing in me).

Thanks to Audrée, who inspires me every day.

Thanks to Guylaine, who was a comfort in my life at a time when I needed it most. Your openness, your listening skills and your deep understanding allowed me to see things differently and to extricate myself from my cocoon.

Thank you to my friends who have seen me very little in the past year given how busy I was with writing and researching this encyclopedia. I hope this book is interesting enough that you can forgive my repeated absences and long silences. (I'll be back soon!)

Thank you to my parents for giving me the chance to do what I wanted in life, even though my journey wasn't straightforward. Thank you for teaching me to be open to others. Thank you for supporting me, no matter what path I took.

Thank you to the teachers of the program in sexology at Université du Québec à Montréal (UQAM), who have allowed me to refine and explore subjects I have been interested in for years.

Thank you to everyone I may have forgotten here.

RESOURCES
(by topic)

Bullying and Cyberbullying

Cyber Civil Rights Initiative: cybercivilrights.org

Stop Bullying: stopbullying.gov

Crisis Lines

Canada Suicide Prevention Service: 1-833-456-4566

Hope for Wellness Helpline (Indigenous mental health support): hopeforwellness.ca

Kids Help Phone: kidshelpphone.ca, 1-800-668-6868

National Domestic Violence Hotline: thehotline.org

National Suicide Prevention Lifeline (US): 1-800-273-TALK (8255)

Teen Line: teenlineonline.org

The Trevor Project (crisis support for LGBTQQIP2SAA+ youth): thetrevorproject.org, 1-866-4-U-TREVOR

Eating Disorders

Eating Disorder Hope: eatingdisorderhope.com

National Eating Disorders Association (NEDA): nationaleatingdisorders.org

Health and Sexuality

AMAZE (sexual education): amaze.org

Disabilities: youth.gov/youth-topics/disabilities

KidsHealth: kidshealth.org

Mental Health Literacy: mentalhealthliteracy.org

Planned Parenthood: plannedparenthood.org

Teen Awareness Group (birth control): teenawareness.net/birth-control

Teen Help (general resources): teenhelp.com

Teen Source (sexual wellness resources): teensource.org

Teen Talk (health education): teentalk.ca

Toxic Shock Syndrome Information Service: toxicshock.com

Young Men's Health: youngmenshealthsite.org

Young Women's Health: youngwomenshealth.org

LGBTQQIP2SAA+ Support

Centers for Disease Control and Prevention, resources for LGBTQQIP2SAA+ youth:
cdc.gov/lgbthealth/youth.htm

GLAAD (transgender resources): glaad.org/transgender/resources

NHS Gender Identity Support: nhs.uk/live-well/healthy-body/trans-teenager

The Trevor Project (crisis support for LGBTQQIP2SAA+ youth):
thetrevorproject.org, 1-866-4-U-TREVOR

Mental Health

Anxiety Canada: anxietycanada.com

Breathr mindfulness app: keltymentalhealth.ca/breathr

Centre for Addiction and Mental Health (CAMH): camh.ca

MindShift CBT app: anxietycanada.com/resources/mindshift-cbt

Mood Disorders Association of Ontario: mooddisorders.ca/faq/teen-depression

SiOS (Self-injury Outreach and Support): sioutreach.org

Sexual Assault

RAINN (Rape, Abuse & Incest National Network): rainn.org

STDs and STIs

HIV/AIDS: US National Library of Medicine: medlineplus.gov/hivaids.html

Teen Help: teenhelp.com/c/std-sti

Substance Abuse

NIDA for Teens (drug awareness): teens.drugabuse.gov

Start Your Recovery (substance misuse): startyourrecovery.org

More Resources

Centre for Youth Crime Prevention: rcmp-grc.gc.ca/en/youth-safety/centre-for-youth-crime-prevention

Youth.gov (interactive tools and resources): youth.gov

Youth Radio: yr.media

For a complete list of references, visit the page for this book at orcabook.com.

INDEX

Page numbers in **bold** indicate the main entry.

CINDY BOYCE

Myriam Daguzan Bernier is the author of the blog *La tête dans le cul* and a regular columnist for ICI Radio-Canada Première's radio show *Moteur de recherche*. She is also a communication specialist and instructor at L'inis, Quebec's national institute of sound and image. Myriam is currently studying sexology at Université du Québec à Montréal and plans to become a sexologist focusing on a feminist and inclusive approach.

BRIAN W. FERRY

Cécile Gariépy is a Montreal-based illustrator. She has illustrated in many different media for clients such as the *New York Times*, Google and *Esquire UK*. Cécile loves images that tell stories, and her playful art puts an emphasis on color, composition and character design.

ORCA
ISSUES

SPARK CHANGE

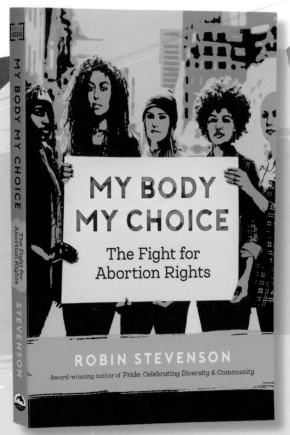

ORCA
ISSUES

MY BODY MY CHOICE

The Fight for Abortion Rights

MY BODY MY CHOICE

The Fight for
Abortion Rights

ROBIN STEVENSON

Award-winning author of *Pride: Celebrating Diversity & Community*

★ "Required reading for
teens of every gender."
—*BOOKLIST*, starred review